Gypsy Stew - 33
Green Chili Sauce - 59
Oysters St. Jacques - 68
Boiled Shrimp Jamima - 78
Green Chili Sauce - 83
Flour Tortillas - 140

THE

Pink Adobe

C O O K B O O K

THE
Pink Adobe
COOKBOOK

Rosalea Murphy

A DELL TRADE PAPERBACK

A DELL TRADE PAPERBACK
Published by
Dell Publishing
a division of
Bantam Doubleday Dell Publishing Group, Inc.
666 Fifth Avenue
New York, New York 10103

Designed by Sheree L. Goodman

The trademark Delacorte Press® is registered in the U.S. Patent and Trademark Office.

ISBN: 0-440-56972-9

Printed in the United States of America
Published simultaneously in Canada

June 1988

10 9 8 7 6 5 4 3

MV

Contents

*To my many friends and patrons, whose encouragement
and enduring support helped The Pink Adobe achieve
a success beyond my dreams.*

Preface

In the summer of 1944 I opened the Pink Adobe Restaurant in the Barrio de Analco, across the street from the San Miguel mission, in Santa Fe, New Mexico. Santa Fe was a lazy, sleepy town then; we bought wood from old men who wandered the streets, slowly leading their supply-laden burros through town. I had never run a restaurant before, never cooked professionally. But I had learned to appreciate the art of cooking creatively during my youth in New Orleans, where I experienced the marvelously complex flavors of Creole cooking.

When "the Pink," as it is known to regulars, opened its doors, it was a modest enterprise. The place seated thirty people if you count those squeezed on the sofa and standing at the counter. It was a real struggle in the early days—I still remember the elation I felt the night we took in $30; I cried, "Wow, this covers half the rent money!"—but, from the moment I started, I knew I'd never let the Pink go.

Our original menu was brief, but even then I used only the finest and freshest ingredients available to create my concoctions. And, fortunately, it wasn't too long before the earliest customers spread the word that the Pink's Dobeburgers, fresh apple pie, and, of all things, French onion soup, were something to experience.

As I traveled over the years I continued to expand the menu, to introduce new dishes to the Pink's customers, and sometimes to the region. I brought chicken enchiladas up from Mexico, and the Pink was the first restaurant to serve seafood in Santa Fe.

The present Pink Adobe is housed in a three-hundred-year-old former barracks a few doors down from the first space I leased those forty-odd years ago. Its walls are thirty-six inches thick, with small windows that were originally placed high to protect against arrows. Six fireplaces cozily keep diners warm during the Santa Fe winter; my paintings and those of my friends decorate the walls. The building is, of course, stuccoed pink.

The recipes currently used at the Pink and the others printed in this cookbook are the direct result of a blending of various cuisines on a Santa Fe palette. It is my hope that you will find my recipes unique, just as the city of Santa Fe is unique. Santa Fe is a focal point of racial meetings. And, in addition to Anglo-American, Hispanic, and Indian cultures, it attracts a colony of anthropologists, scientists, artists, writers, and moviemakers far out of proportion to its size. These also contribute through educated tastes and lives of diverse experience an influence in terms of cooking.

Because I came to Santa Fe from New Orleans, via San Antonio, it is quite natural that my recipes are also sometimes influenced by the Creole and Cajun. While the origin of some of the recipes in this cookbook may puzzle both French and Spanish chefs de cuisine (as so many works of art create bewilderment), I am confident that you'll find the results inspiring.

Thus, from my earliest memories in the good food land of Louisiana, from newfound knowledge in the Land of Enchantment that is New Mexico, from a natural love of good eating, and, finally and most important, from a very strong compulsion to create dishes of my own, has evolved *The Pink Adobe Cookbook*.

Rosalea Murphy

Santa Fe
May 1988

Notes on Recipes and Ingredients

The collection of eclectic recipes in this book is meant to be a guide rather than a "follow-to-the-letter" dictatorial message. Seasonings and flavors can certainly be changed to the tastes of each individual cook. Creativity in the kitchen is a true art; after learning basic techniques, you should feel free to experiment so as to achieve a personal and unique style of your own.

I think the overriding attitude of all good cooks should be an insistence on quality. Fresh foods should be used whenever possible; when in doubt, choose the best. I'm not a believer in sparing expense when it comes to cooking, although many recipes herein won't prove expensive.

Substitutions, too, should be made only with ingredients of equal quality. Shrimp, crab, and lobster are all adaptable to the same sauce. Sherry and Madeira are interchangeable, as are rum and brandy. When a recipe calls for white wine, I always use dry vermouth, but you may have your own favorite. Follow your instincts and use your imagination.

Remember that eating, too, is an art. So, when preparing a

meal, keep in mind that it is a salutary advantage to pamper your palate as well as that of your guests.

Think of each meal as a special celebration. Offer ideas that capture the spirit of the occasion—whether it is a picnic, a barbecue, or an intimate sit-down dinner. The underlying purpose is to please and pamper your guests. Many diners today are bored with traditional foods. Take advantage of artistic license and mix the old with the new to create interest for all concerned.

By bringing pleasure to your kitchen and enjoyment to the dining room, it is certain that both you and your guests will become gastronomically wiser.

How to Use This Book

There's nothing unusual about the way this book is organized; the chapter titles speak for themselves. However, don't let the chapter divisions limit your menu planning. The fact that Shrimp Rémoulade, for example, is given in the appetizers chapter does not mean it wouldn't be a wonderful entree for a special luncheon or a light dinner on a steamy day. Likewise, a soup doesn't have to be served as a soup course; the chapter on soups includes some choices that are hearty enough to be the centerpiece of a cozy winter meal in front of the fireplace. As you will adapt the recipes to suit your individual tastes, you should combine recipes to plan menus to your liking.

In addition to the usual categories of food in this book, I have included a section on beverages and ideas and menus for southwestern entertainment. Our lifestyle in New Mexico is casual and relaxed. It has been said that nowhere in the world is the sky bluer or the air clearer. Needless to say, this environment lends itself beautifully to informal entertainment under the sky.

Few of the recipes in this book require long, complicated preparation, though many have make-ahead steps that allow you to do some or all of the cooking in advance.

Serving suggestions and compatible accompaniments are given with many of the recipes, but again, let your own preferences be your guide. I've also included recommendations for wine selections with many of the entrees. These were provided by Jeff

Thurston, the very knowledgeable wine steward at the Pink Adobe. And, of course, champagne is a favorite; served with appetizers through dessert, it is a satisfying option. For hot, spicy foods, beer is a wise choice. At the Pink Adobe, the Mexican beer Corona is the most in demand.

Ingredients

As I stated earlier, using the best quality ingredients is paramount. While I have given canned and frozen alternatives for fresh ingredients in many recipes, I strongly advise that you use the fresh foods whenever possible. The difference in flavor and texture is well worth any additional effort required.

The same rule applies when a sauce or other recipe is called for in another recipe. For example, I've included a recipe for homemade mayonnaise in Chapter 4. Wherever mayonnaise is called for, you may, of course, substitute a good quality store-bought mayonnaise, but the homemade version is far superior.

Almost all of the ingredients specified in the recipes should be available in supermarkets, depending on the size and location of your community. You may need to do a little hunting to find a few of the ingredients; check your local gourmet or specialty food shop. See page xiii for some additional help.

The following information should answer any questions you may have about any of the ingredients called for in the recipes.

• Chiles. Although chile is used throughout the world in numerous cuisines such as Cajun, Szechwan, and Indonesian, it seems to be most basic to New Mexican cooking. Because there are so many different types, intensities, and flavors of chiles in the Southwest, their frequent use assures piquancy without necessarily creating repetitious flavors.

In New Mexico, the first crop of chile is harvested in July, when it is still green, and remains on the roadside stands until the first frost of the season. The second crop of chile, picked in early fall, is allowed to fully ripen and turn red.

No scene is more typical of New Mexico in the fall than ripe, red chile pods sun-drying and hanging in ristras (tied together in strands) on the walls and vigas of old adobe houses. When dried, the red pods are either ground into powder or left whole to be used in a sauce.

Since chile will vary both in taste and shape depending on what region it was grown in, it is helpful to know what types can be substituted for flavor and amount of pungency desired. I use the following (of the hundreds of chiles available) in my recipes:

The hottest chile native to New Mexico is the *Hatch*, grown in the town of Hatch in southern New Mexico—the Las Cruces area. It is thick-fleshed, about five to seven inches long and two inches wide, and bright green in the spring; bright red in the fall.

The Española valley in the north is the home of the milder *Española* chiles, which resemble the Hatch in appearance.

Jalapeño chiles are small, narrow, dark green or sometimes yellow, and extremely hot; hotter than the New Mexican Hatch. They are native to Mexico, but are now grown throughout the Southwest.

Serrano chiles, even smaller than the jalapeño with a medium-green color and one pointed end are also very hot (comparable to the jalapeño).

Anaheim chiles, grown in California, are very flavorful and mild. They are long and narrow with one pointed end.

The *ancho*, *mulato*, and *pasillo* chiles are all from Mexico. Their flavor is distinctive and mild; all are oblong, wide (about three to four inches) and dark green.

Chile pequin is made from the peppers found on the very pretty, very petite little bush many southwesterners grow at home. These tiny yellow and green peppers, when dried and crushed, are extremely hot. If the chile you are using is not hot enough for your taste, add a teaspoon or two of chile pequin—slowly.

Many of the above chiles can be found in a well-stocked supermarket; most are available in Hispanic markets. If you have trouble locating specific chiles, you will find the sources listed below helpful. These chiles and many others can be found in a variety of forms:

Frozen chile, both red and green, is available in many supermarkets. You can prepare and freeze chiles yourself (see page xiv).

Whole and chopped chiles, as well as various red and green salsas, are available in cans and jars.

Dried red chile can be found in three forms: chili powder, chile flakes, and crushed chile. Chili powder is readily available in most supermarkets and food specialty stores. While powder usually comes in regular and "Mexican hot" versions, crushed chile or flaked chile will generally still pack more of a punch. The recipes herein specify the form of chile required, but I do encourage experimentation. I like the coarser texture of a dish made with crushed chile better than the milder, smoother result of chili powder.

Chile jelly is available in Hispanic markets and in many supermarkets.

As you continue to cook southwestern dishes, you may wish to experiment with the new tastes of different chiles and chili powders. I contact the following suppliers whenever I have trouble finding chile products; you can find interesting products and valuable information through these sources:

Jose's Best Tortilla Factory
P.O. Box 5525
Santa Fe, New Mexico 87501

Jackalope (This is a small supply house, but one of the very
   few that will ship you a ristra.)
2820 Cerrillos Road
Santa Fe, New Mexico 87501

Lujan's Place (This small supply house specializes in unusual,
   regional herbs and spices.)
218 Galisteo
Santa Fe, New Mexico 87501

Casados Farms
P.O. Box 852
San Juan Pueblo, New Mexico 87566

Bueno Brand Food Products
2001 Fourth N.W.
Albuquerque, New Mexico 87102

Preparing Chiles for Cooking

The skin of fresh chiles is very tough, so chiles must be peeled before being used in any recipe. Roasting these chiles loosens the skin for peeling. While there are many different ways to roast and peel a chile, I have found the following method to be the most efficient and convenient.

To roast and peel green chiles: *Always use gloves when handling chiles!* Select smooth pods with well-rounded shoulders. Place 12 pods on a cookie sheet under broiler about 3 inches below broiler unit. Leave the oven door open while broiling. Turn pods frequently as they begin to blister. When completely blistered (entire pod should be charred but not burned), remove from broiler. Wrap in a damp, clean dishtowel and allow to steam for 10 minutes. Remove stem end, scrape out seeds (if desired; much of the pepper's potency is in the seeds), and peel outer skin downward.

You can freeze roasted and peeled chiles; in fact, while the best possible result is reached when chiles have not been frozen, I find fresh, frozen chiles far superior to canned in any recipe.

• Tomatoes. While several years ago, fresh tomatoes were virtually impossible to find in the winter, now hothouse tomatoes are available year-round. In the peak of their season, nothing can replace the flavor of sun-ripened tomatoes.

To peel tomatoes: Immerse tomato for approximately 30 seconds in boiling water. The skin should then slide off easily. (If not, immerse for another 30 seconds.)

• Horseradish. Horseradish provides a different type of piquancy from chiles and is worth becoming familiar with if you haven't used it much before. Bottles of prepared horseradish usually are stocked in your supermarket's dairy section, as it needs to be refrigerated. As with chiles, you can choose the level of hotness desired. Not all brands indicate the level of hotness on the label, so you might have to become familiar with certain brands by tasting them.

• Herbs. In the recipes I have specified whether herbs should be fresh or dried. Most recipes call for dried herbs because they are available year-round, but if you have access to fresh herbs never hesitate to use them instead. Simply double or triple (depending on the strength of the fresh herbs) the quantity listed for dried and chop fine.

• Cilantro. If you're familiar with Mexican or Far Eastern cooking, you've probably used cilantro. It's simply the fresh leaves of the coriander plant, and it has a unique pungency. Find it in the produce section of your market; it looks something like flat-leaf parsley or watercress.

• **Lettuce.** You should never use a knife on lettuce or other tender greens such as fresh spinach. Cutting them bruises them. Instead, tear the leaves into bite-size pieces with your hands.

• **Bell peppers.** Bell peppers come in a veritable rainbow of colors these days. The most widely available are green and red. Where color is not specified in a recipe, you should use green, though the slightly sweeter red peppers may be substituted.

• **Bouquet garni.** Bouquet garni is a mixture of herbs used in French cooking; Premixed versions are available in the supermarket (I like Spice Island).

• **Corn.** Corn is a southwestern staple, and when it is in season, you should use fresh corn. The number of kernels you'll get from an ear will vary quite a bit depending on the size of the cob. A single ear could yield anywhere from ¼ cup to 1 cup; assume an average of ½ cup per ear unless the corn is particularly small or large.

You'll find tips on other ingredients in the recipes themselves.

Appetizers

A good meal should start with tempting taste teasers. They should be spicy or salty enough to create a small thirst and, in their irresistible way, be forerunners of delectable dishes of food to follow. Of course, one can always plan a feast of a variety of appetizers.

Santa Fe Layered Bean Dip

YIELD: 12 SERVINGS

2   cups cooked pinto beans (1 cup when dry)
1   tablespoon minced onion
1   cup grated sharp cheddar cheese
6   drops Tabasco sauce
     Salt to taste
2   tablespoons bacon or ham fat

3   medium ripe avocados
2   tablespoons fresh lemon juice
½   teaspoon salt
½   teaspoon freshly ground black pepper

1   cup dairy sour cream
½   cup mayonnaise (page 54)
1   1¼-ounce package taco seasoning mix

1   7-ounce can pitted ripe olives, drained and chopped
3   medium tomatoes, peeled (page xiv) and chopped coarse
1   cup chopped green onions
     Tostados (page 3)

Drain and mash beans. Add onion, cheese, and Tabasco and blend well. Salt to taste. Heat the fat in a large iron skillet and add the bean mixture. Stir until cheese is melted and the whole mixture is bubbling. Set aside.

Peel, pit, and mash avocados in bowl with lemon juice, ½ teaspoon salt, and pepper. In a separate bowl combine sour cream, mayonnaise, and taco seasoning.

To assemble, spread half of the bean dip on a large shallow serving platter. Top with half of the avocado mixture and half of the sour cream mixture. Sprinkle with half of the olives, tomatoes, and green onions. Repeat with another layer of mashed beans, avocado, sour cream, olives, tomatoes, and onions. Serve with tostados.

Marinated Garbanzos

2   cups cooked garbanzos (see Note)
1   clove garlic
½   cup olive oil
3   tablespoons tarragon vinegar
3   tablespoons red wine
½   teaspoon salt
¼   teaspoon freshly ground black pepper

Drain the garbanzos well. Run the garlic through a press or crush and mince thoroughly. Combine all ingredients and marinate for at least 4 hours (preferably overnight), stirring from time to time. Serve cold.

NOTE: Garbanzos are also known as chick-peas in some parts of the United States. They can be bought canned or dry. If dry, soak over-night and cook like any other dried beans.

Tostados

Here in New Mexico we have blue corn tortillas, made from blue corn, as well as yellow corn tortillas. Corn tortillas (yellow or blue) can be substituted.

1   dozen Flour Tortillas (page 140)
     Fat for deep frying (enough to submerge tortillas in pan)
     Salt to taste

Cut the tortillas into quarters. Heat the fat in a deep skillet until very hot and drop in the quartered tortillas a few at a time. Salt lightly.

Peanut Chicken Wings

YIELD: 15–20 SERVINGS

- 50 chicken wings
- 2 12-ounce bottles beer
- 1 cup molasses
- ½ cup creamy peanut butter
- ½ cup fresh lemon juice
- ½ cup Worcestershire sauce
- ¼ cup prepared mustard
- 1 teaspoon salt
- 2 tablespoons chili powder
- ¼ cup chopped fresh parsley, for garnish
- 1–2 lemons, sliced thin, for garnish

Preheat oven to 450°F. Remove and discard tips from wings and cut each wing in half at joint. Combine remaining ingredients except parsley and lemon slices in a large saucepan. Cook over low heat for about 15 minutes, until reduced and thickened to the consistency of thick gravy. Place wings in a large roasting pan and cover with sauce. Turn until each wing is well coated. Bake for 15–20 minutes. Serve on large platter. Garnish with parsley and lemon slices.

Nachos

YIELD: 12–15 SERVINGS

- 1 pound homemade Tostados (recipe below), or 1 16-ounce package corn tortilla chips
- 2 cups Monterey Jack cheese, grated
- 1 cup Salsa Diabolique (page 22)

Place chips on large baking sheet. Sprinkle cheese evenly over chips. Cover cheese with salsa. Broil until cheese melts, approximately 2–3 minutes.

Fiesta Caviar Pie

YIELD: 6 SERVINGS

The beauty and elegance of this make-ahead appetizer will delight your guests.

6   hard-cooked eggs, chopped coarse
3   tablespoons mayonnaise (page 54)
1½ cups minced green onions
8   ounces cream cheese
½   cup dairy sour cream
2   ounces black caviar
1   ounce each white and red salmon caviar
1–2 lemons, cut into wedges, for garnish
     Few sprigs fresh parsley, for garnish
     Brown bread—pumpernickel, rye, or both

Combine eggs with mayonnaise. Spread over bottom of well-greased 8-inch springform pan. Sprinkle onions over eggs. In food processor blend cream cheese and sour cream until soft and spreadable. With a wet spatula, spread cheese mixture over onions. Cover and chill at least 3 hours or overnight. Before serving, arrange the three caviars in a pretty design on top of cheese mixture, spreading to edges. Run knife around pan sides to loosen. Lift mixture out of pan and transfer to large platter. Garnish with lemon and parsley. Surround with buttered brown bread cut into triangular pieces.

Pink Adobe Guacamole

YIELD: 6 SERVINGS

2	large ripe avocados
1	clove garlic, minced
1	small onion, minced
½	cup peeled, seeded, and chopped fresh green chiles (page xiv) or 1 4-ounce can green chiles, chopped (2 cans if you're a real southwesterner)
½	teaspoon salt
1	tablespoon mayonnaise (page 54)
1–3	tablespoons lemon juice, to taste
1	large lettuce leaf, for garnish
	Paprika, for garnish
	Tomato slices, for garnish
	Tostados (page 3)

NOTE: The result should be like cool chartreuse velvet, not liquid at all. Taste often. The flavor should be just a little hot and a little tart. If the chiles are too mild, they can be pepped up with Tabasco sauce.

Peel and remove pit from the avocados. Mash with a silver fork until the pulp is very smooth. Blend in garlic, onion, chiles, and salt. Mix in the mayonnaise and stir in the lemon juice. Serve nestled with a lettuce leaf in your prettiest shallow bowl; garnish with paprika and surround with tomato slices and tostado chips for dipping.

Conjurer's Olives

YIELD: 6 SERVINGS

This appetizer takes several days to prepare, to give the olives time to soak up the mysterious, elusive flavor of the marinade.

- 1   clove garlic, halved
- 1   16-ounce can ripe green olives, drained
- 1   cup olive oil
- ½   cup dry sherry
- ⅛   teaspoon each dried thyme,
            pickling spice,
            dried basil,
            dried marjoram,
            ground cloves,
            dried oregano
- 1   bay leaf
- 1   clove garlic, crushed
- ½   lemon

Rub a deep crockery bowl well with the halved garlic clove. Then put in the drained olives and cover with a mixture of the olive oil and sherry. Rub the herbs and mix in. Add bay leaf, garlic, and lemon juice. Gently turn the olives over until they are well coated. Marinate at room temperature for at least two days and up to four days. The olives can be stored in the refrigerator for a week.

Lime-Horseradish Dip

- 1   6-ounce jar lime marmalade
- 1   5-ounce jar prepared hot horseradish

Combine marmalade and horseradish and serve with pork cubes.

Smoked Salmon Ball

YIELD: 10–15 SERVINGS

2   16-ounce cans red sockeye salmon
1   8-ounce package cream cheese, softened
1   clove garlic, pressed
½   cup small-curd cottage cheese
¼   cup minced onion
½   cup minced fresh or canned green chile
½   teaspoon dried thyme
½   teaspoon ground coriander
¼   teaspoon Tabasco sauce
    Few drops Hickory Liquid Smoke
1   cup chopped fresh parsley
1   cup chopped piñons (pine nuts)

Drain salmon. Mash salmon, complete with bones, in food processor. Combine remaining ingredients except parsley and piñons. Stir together with salmon until pureed. Form into ball and chill for several hours. Roll in parsley and nuts. Serve surrounded with chips or crackers.

Chili Peanuts

YIELD: 6 SERVINGS

1   clove garlic
2   tablespoons peanut oil
1   pound roasted unsalted peanuts
1½   teaspoons salt
1   tablespoon chili powder
½   teaspoon cayenne pepper
1   teaspoon fresh lemon juice

Mash garlic and sauté in the peanut oil in a medium skillet over moderate heat. Stir in remaining ingredients and cook for 2 minutes. Let cool and serve at room temperature.

Shrimp Rémoulade

YIELD: 6 SERVINGS

Here's a classic French recipe with a Creole twist.

- 1 cup finely chopped fresh parsley
- 1 cup finely chopped green onions
- ½ cup Creole Mustard, recipe below (Dijon mustard may be substituted, though the taste will not be quite the same.)
- ¾ cup French Dressing (page 53)
  Salt and freshly ground black pepper to taste
- 36 medium shrimp, cooked, peeled, and deveined
- 2 cups shredded lettuce
- ¼ cup chopped fresh parsley, for garnish
- ¼ cup chopped black olives, for garnish

Mix parsley, green onions, and mustard to a paste. Add French Dressing and mix well with a whisk. Add salt and pepper to taste and more French Dressing if too dry. Add shrimp to marinade; marinate in refrigerator about an hour. Divide shredded lettuce on 6 small plates. Divide shrimp evenly among plates and pour marinade over each. Garnish with chopped parsley and chopped olives. Serve as first course.

Creole Mustard

- ¼ cup Dijon mustard
- ¼ cup prepared horseradish

Blend together.

Gingered Pork Cubes with Lime-Horseradish Dip

YIELD: 8 SERVINGS

While this recipe isn't influenced by the Southwest, I developed it to serve at cocktail parties and it is always a hit. We can tire of chile even in Santa Fe!

1½	pounds boneless pork tenderloin, cut into 1-inch cubes
3	tablespoons soy sauce
1	small clove garlic, pressed
½	teaspoon freshly ground black pepper
½	teaspoon sugar
¼	teaspoon ground ginger
1	tablespoon peanut oil

Mix pork with other ingredients. Place in glass bowl and cover. Let stand at room temperature for 2 hours, turning meat several times. Preheat oven to 325°F. Spread pork in single layer on a 12-by-9-by-2-inch baking pan and bake for 1 hour. Turn several times during cooking. Pour off fat and place pork mixture in a chafing dish over low heat. Serve with picks and a bowl of Lime-Horseradish Dip (page 7) next to chafing dish.

Oyster Frivolities

YIELD: 6 SERVINGS

I brought this tempter with me from Louisiana.

½ pound butter
3 ounces caviar (see Note)
15 thin-sliced whole wheat or rye bread rounds (about the size of silver dollars)
1 2-ounce can anchovy fillets
1 pint shucked oysters, drained
 Fresh lemon juice
 Freshly ground black pepper to taste

Put ¼ pound butter in food processor, add the caviar, and blend. Butter half of the bread rounds with this. Now make a paste of the remaining butter and the anchovies, mashed, covering the other half of the bread rounds with this mixture. Place an oyster on each buttered round and sprinkle with a few drops of lemon juice and a little black pepper.

NOTE: *There are many grades of caviar available; generally speaking, the better the grade (and, unfortunately, the more expensive), the better this treat will taste.*

Rosemary Walnuts

YIELD: 6 SERVINGS

I often put these in a jar with a tight-fitting lid and give them as Christmas presents.

2 cups shelled whole walnuts
2½ tablespoons butter, melted
2 teaspoons crumbled dried rosemary
1½ teaspoons salt
½ teaspoon cayenne pepper

Preheat oven to 350°F. Place walnuts in a single layer in a shallow pan. Mix together remaining ingredients and pour over walnuts. Roast in oven about 10 minutes, until browned, shaking occasionally.

Sauces, Dips, and Relishes

Sauces give that added "extra" to almost any dish—from appetizers to desserts. Pasta alone can be boring, but with an imaginative sauce, it can metamorphose into a ravishing winner. Relishes and dips add excitement and zest and are a harmonious companion for many foods.

Pink Adobe Apricot Chutney

YIELD: 1 QUART

NOTE: This chutney goes well with any meat; it's especially good with roast pork or lamb.

In northern New Mexico the fruit crop is usually very bountiful. In a good year there is an overabundance of apricots, apples, and peaches. One of the many things to do with the fruit is to make chutney. Use only one fruit or a combination.

2	cups brown sugar
1	cup granulated sugar
1½	cups red wine vinegar
2	tablespoons mustard seed
1	teaspoon ground ginger
2	teaspoons salt
3	tablespoons finely chopped jalapeño pepper
1	teaspoon crushed red chile pepper
7	cups peeled, pitted, and coarsely chopped fresh apricots, apples, or peaches, or a combination
1	whole lemon, chopped, with peel
½	cup dried currants
4	ounces crystallized ginger, chopped
4	(2 pounds) yellow onions, sliced very thin
2	cloves garlic, minced

Bring the sugars and vinegar to a boil in large soup pot. Add the mustard seed, ginger, salt, and peppers and bring to a simmer. Add the fruit and remaining ingredients and simmer, uncovered, for 1½ hours. Cool and store in refrigerator for up to two weeks.

Pink Adobe Barbecue Sauce

YIELD: 1 QUART

This is a very spicy and hot sauce. Delicious!

4	slices bacon, cut into ½-inch pieces
1	cup chopped onion
1	clove garlic, crushed
1	14-ounce bottle catsup
¼	cup vinegar
¼	cup lemon juice
½	cup Worcestershire sauce
¼	cup white corn syrup (Karo)
1	tablespoon molasses
¼	cup brown sugar
½	teaspoon cayenne pepper
1	teaspoon chili powder
1	teaspoon red chile flakes
1	teaspoon paprika
½	teaspoon dry mustard
1	teaspoon salt
1	teaspoon barbecue spice
½	teaspoon Tabasco sauce
1	cup pineapple juice
1	capful Liquid Smoke (more as desired)

In heavy 4-quart stockpot, fry bacon. When crisp, remove and drain on paper towels. Sauté onion and garlic in bacon fat until transparent. Add remaining ingredients, except pineapple juice and Liquid Smoke. Add fried bacon. Bring to a slow boil and simmer for 10 minutes. Add pineapple juice and Liquid Smoke. Stir and cook for 2 minutes. Taste. If a smokier taste is desired, add a little more Liquid Smoke.

Black Bean Sauce

YIELD: 6 SERVINGS

This sauce is excellent with steak, roast beef, or pork.

4	tablespoons olive oil
¾	cup finely diced onion
¼	cup each finely diced green, red, and yellow bell peppers
1	teaspoon sliced fresh jalapeño pepper
2	cups chopped fresh tomatoes
2	cups cooked black beans
2	tablespoons fresh lime juice
½	teaspoon sugar
	Salt and freshly ground black pepper to taste

Heat oil in a 12-inch sauté pan. Sauté onion, bell peppers, and jalapeño for 5 minutes, stirring constantly. Add tomatoes and stir. Add cooked beans and cook for 2 minutes. Remove from heat and stir in lime juice, sugar, salt, and pepper.

Cranberry Relish

YIELD: APPROXIMATELY 5 CUPS

I serve this delicious relish at the Pink every Thanksgiving and Christmas; it's a great accompaniment for roast pork as well as the Thanksgiving fowls.

2	cups fresh cranberries
2	oranges, cut into eighths, unpeeled
2	cups sugar
1	cup pecan pieces

In food processor fitted with steel blade, process cranberries and oranges with an on/off movement until chopped somewhat coarse. Transfer to mixing bowl and stir in sugar first, then pecan pieces. Let rest for several hours before using.

Blender Hollandaise Sauce

YIELD: 1 CUP

This quick and easy Hollandaise enhances Scallops Piñon (page 72) and Poached Salmon (page 74). It is also delicious on simply steamed green vegetables and other plain fish preparations.

3	egg yolks
2	tablespoons fresh lemon juice
1/8	teaspoon cayenne pepper
1/4	teaspoon salt
1/4	pound butter, melted

Place egg yolks, lemon juice, cayenne pepper, and salt in a blender. Blend on and off until combined. Heat butter to boiling, but don't burn. Slowly pour hot butter into blender on high speed. Continue blending only until the sauce thickens, about 30 seconds. Use at once or keep sauce warm in the top of a double boiler, over warm, not boiling, water.

Corn Relish

YIELD: APPROXIMATELY 3 CUPS

2   cups cooked fresh yellow corn kernels (about 4 ears) or 16 ounces frozen or canned corn
½   cup roasted, peeled, and chopped fresh green chile (page xiv)
1   teaspoon chopped fresh jalapeño pepper
¼   cup chopped celery
¼   cup finely chopped onion
¼   teaspoon freshly ground black pepper
1   teaspoon chili powder
¼   teaspoon dried oregano
½   teaspoon minced fresh cilantro
¼   cup cider vinegar
½   cup olive oil

Combine all ingredients in a large bowl. Chill several hours before serving.

Fresh Red Chile Sauce

YIELD: 1–1½ CUPS

This sauce will enliven countless foods. Try it over eggs, with pork, and of course, with Tostados.

15   large fresh red chiles
1   quart boiling water
1   clove garlic, peeled
1   teaspoon salt
1   teaspoon dried oregano
½   teaspoon ground cumin

Preheat oven to 350°F. Remove stems and seeds from chiles. Wash under running water. Spread on baking sheet and roast for 5 minutes. Transfer to large bowl. Cover with boiling water. Let stand for 10 minutes. Transfer chiles to blender and add enough water just to cover. Add seasonings and blend to a smooth paste.

Green Chile Relish

YIELD: APPROXIMATELY 4 CUPS

Great on hamburgers!

½	cup cider vinegar
½	cup sugar
1	tablespoon dried dill weed
1	tablespoon dill seed
1	tablespoon mustard seed
1	tablespoon chopped fresh cilantro
2	cloves garlic, halved
3	cups freshly roasted, peeled, and chopped green chiles (page xiv) or 1 27-ounce can green chiles, drained and chopped

In saucepan over low heat, combine all the ingredients except the chiles. Mix together well. Bring to a slow boil. Remove from heat. Add chiles and mix well. Refrigerate.

Fresh Green Chiles with Lime Marmalade

YIELD: 6 SERVINGS

The white bread and butter tame the hotness of the chiles. Delicious!

- ½ teaspoon dried oregano
- ½ teaspoon salt
- 1 clove garlic, peeled
- ¼ cup olive oil
- 1 cup lime marmalade
- 10 fresh green chiles, roasted and peeled (page xiv)

Process the oregano, salt, and garlic in a food processor until garlic is mashed. Add olive oil and process until smooth. With on/off movements, add marmalade. Split each whole chile into 4 strips. Remove seeds. Place in a 10-by-15-by-2-inch glass dish. Pour marmalade mixture over chiles and marinate overnight. Serve with buttered fresh white bread.

Tartar Sauce

YIELD: 1¼ CUPS

The mayonnaise must be of good quality for this recipe. Never use salad dressing. This is the perfect sauce for Fried Shrimp Louisiane (page 76), but also try it with any of your favorite fried seafood dishes.

1   cup mayonnaise (page 54)
1   tablespoon finely minced onion
1   teaspoon finely minced parsley
1   teaspoon capers
½   teaspoon fresh lemon juice
1   teaspoon finely minced sweet pickles

Mix all ingredients well.

Tomato Sauce

YIELD: 6 SERVINGS

Serve over Dixieland Chicken Roll (page 88) or over pasta for a mild sauce.

1   small carrot, chopped fine
1   small onion, chopped fine
1   clove garlic, minced
3   tablespoons butter
2½   cups cooked tomatoes or 1 20-ounce can stewed tomatoes
¼   cup flour
1   pinch dried thyme
1   teaspoon sugar
1½   cups chicken stock

Sauté carrot, onion, and garlic in butter until wilted and soft. Add the tomatoes and sift in the flour. Add thyme, sugar, and stock and bring to a boil, stirring constantly. Boil for 3 or 4 minutes. Reduce heat and cook over low heat for 1 hour, stirring occasionally. Put in food processor and process until smooth. Return to saucepan and bring back to a boil; cook 5 minutes.

Salsa Diabolique

NOTE: A bull shot is 4 ounces beef consommé plus 1½ ounces vodka.

6   (3 pounds) ripe tomatoes, peeled and chopped coarse (page xiv)
¼   cup each coarsely chopped red and yellow onions
2   shallots, chopped
1   3½-ounce can pickled jalapeño peppers, chopped
1   ounce bull shot mix (see Note)
1   teaspoon chopped fresh cilantro or ground coriander
1   teaspoon ground cumin
1   teaspoon salt
1   tablespoon fresh lime juice

Combine all ingredients in a large bowl. Let stand at least 1 hour to allow all ingredients to blend. Serve with tortilla chips.

Soups and Stews

In my opinion, there is no kitchen aroma more pleasurable than that of a pot of homemade soup simmering on the stove. Nor is there any food to make one feel more nurtured than a steaming bowl of soup. Some of the soups and stews in the recipes that follow are hearty enough to serve as a meal in themselves. Just add a salad and a light fruit dessert.

Cold Soups

Avocado-Jalapeño Soup

YIELD: 6 SERVINGS

- ¼ cup butter
- ¼ cup flour
- 2 cups milk
- 2 cups half-and-half
- 1 teaspoon salt
  Grated rind of 1 lime
- 3 ripe avocados
- 1 tablespoon fresh lemon juice
- ½ teaspoon very finely chopped onion
- 1 teaspooon finely chopped jalapeño pepper
- ¼ cup cream, whipped, for garnish
- ½ teaspoon chili powder, for garnish

Melt butter in top of double boiler, add flour, and blend with a wire whisk. In a medium saucepan, bring milk and half-and-half to a boil. Add to butter-flour mixture and whisk thoroughly. Add salt and lime rind, stirring until mixture thickens. Mash 2 of the avocados and add to soup, mixing thoroughly. Add lemon juice, onion, and jalapeño. Chill for several hours or overnight. Just before serving, cube remaining avocado. Serve soup in chilled bowls and garnish with cubed avocado, dab of whipped cream, and chili powder.

Pink Adobe Gazpacho

YIELD: 6 SERVINGS

1	large onion, quartered
1	clove garlic, peeled
5	large fresh tomatoes, peeled (page xiv)
1	small cucumber, peeled
2	tablespoons each chopped fresh parsley, vinegar, paprika
3	tablespoons olive oil
1	16-ounce can beef broth
	Salt and freshly ground black pepper to taste
	Croutons, for garnish
2	tablespoons chopped black olives, for garnish
2	tablespoons finely chopped green bell pepper, for garnish
2	tablespoons finely chopped peeled cucumber, for garnish

Blend onion and garlic in a food processor or blender. Add tomatoes and cucumber. Blend until mushy. Add parsley, vinegar, paprika, oil, broth, and salt and pepper to taste. Blend well. Chill overnight and serve very cold. Garnish each serving with croutons, olives, bell pepper, and cucumber.

Hot Soups

Brie with Green Chile Soup

YIELD: 6 SERVINGS

This soup is a very rich and smooth beginning for a southwestern meal. American Brie is now available, and I find it equal, if not superior, to French Brie (due to a shorter traveling time from Wisconsin).

¾ cup chopped onion
½ cup chopped celery
4 tablespoons butter
2 tablespoons flour
1 pint (16 ounces) half-and-half
1 16-ounce can chicken broth
½ pound Brie, cut into small pieces
1 cup roasted, peeled, and chopped fresh green chiles (page xiv) or 2 4-ounce cans green chiles, chopped
   Salt and freshly ground black pepper to taste

Sauté onion and celery in butter in large saucepan. Stir in flour. Using a whisk, slowly add half-and-half and chicken broth. Stir constantly until blended. Add Brie and whisk until melted. Add chiles, salt, and pepper. Ladle soup into bowls and serve hot.

Black Bean Soup

YIELD: 8–10 SERVINGS

1	pound dried black beans
1	medium bell pepper or fresh green chile, chopped
¼	cup olive oil
3	large onions, chopped
4	cloves garlic, minced
4	14½-ounce cans beef broth
1½	pounds meaty ham hock
1	tablespoon ground cumin
1	tablespoon dried oregano
½	teaspoon dried thyme
1	bay leaf
½	cup chopped pickled jalapeños
2	tablespoons dry sherry
	Salt and freshly ground black pepper to taste
	Diced tomato, chopped green onions, sliced hard-cooked eggs, sour cream, for garnish

Wash beans. Cover with water, add chopped green pepper, and soak overnight. Drain beans. Heat oil in frying pan. Add onions and garlic. Sauté three minutes; add beans. Cover with broth, add ham hock, and simmer for 1 hour. Add seasonings, jalapeño, sherry, and salt and pepper and continue to cook for another 1½ hours. To thicken soup, remove about 1 cup of beans from pot, mash, and return to pot. Stir well. Taste for seasoning. Ladle soup into bowls. Garnish with tomato, green onion, sliced egg, and sour cream.

Sopa de Albondigas
(Mexican Meatball Soup)

YIELD: 6–8 SERVINGS AS A MEAL;
UP TO 20 SERVINGS IF ONE OF SEVERAL COURSES

Serve with a green salad for a hearty southwestern meal.

Meatballs

2	pounds round steak and 1 pound pork shoulder, ground together
3	eggs
1	large fresh green chile, chopped fine
3	bunches green onions, chopped fine
3	sprigs fresh mint
½	clove garlic, chopped fine
1½	cups cornmeal
¼	cup chopped fresh parsley
¾	teaspoon dried sage
½	teaspoon ground cloves
⅓	cup solidly packed drained and chopped tomatoes

Soup Stock

3	10-ounce cans condensed beef bouillon
1	cup tomato juice
1	fresh or canned hot green chile, chopped fine
1	large pinch chopped fresh parsley
1	pinch dried thyme
1	clove garlic, minced
	Salt and freshly ground black pepper to taste

Prepare the meatballs: Mix all ingredients together, in the order listed above. When well mixed, pinch off pieces and roll into tiny, marble-sized balls. You should end up with about 150 little meatballs. Set aside.

Prepare Soup Stock: Add all soup ingredients to 6 quarts of water. Bring to a boil, then drop in the meatballs, a few at a time, so that they do not stick to each other. Cover tightly and simmer for an hour. It may be necessary to add more water while cooking.

French Onion Soup

YIELD: 6 SERVINGS

The fact that this classic is not southwestern in origin does not stop Santa Feans and visitors from ordering it again and again at the Pink Adobe. With a salad from Chapter 4 and good-quality French bread, it makes a hearty supper that will keep away the winter chill.

¼ pound butter
6 large white onions, peeled and sliced paper-thin (see Note)
3 quarts strong beef broth
Salt to taste
Croutons
Freshly grated Parmesan cheese

Melt the butter in a large pot and, when it begins to heat, add the onions, stirring constantly until they are golden and clear but not at all burned or crisp. Add beef broth. Salt to taste and simmer for 20 minutes. Fill pottery casseroles or French onion soup bowls with the soup. Put croutons in each bowl and sprinkle with Parmesan cheese. Place bowls in hot oven until cheese melts.

NOTE: Onions peeled under cold water won't make you cry.

Mucho Frijoles Soup

NOTE: Some specialty food shops carry 1-pound packages of mixed dried beans. A good mixture is black beans, kidney beans, and garbanzos. To this you can add dried peas, pinto beans, dried limas, or any combination you desire. Just mix enough to equal 1 pound or 2 cups.

YIELD: 6 SERVINGS

2   cups dried beans (see Note)
1½ teaspoons salt
1   large onion, chopped
1   clove garlic, crushed
1½ pounds meaty ham hock
2   cups chopped fresh tomatoes
1   jalapeño pepper, chopped (optional)
3   tablespoons fresh lemon juice
1   teaspoon freshly ground black pepper
2   cups water or chicken stock

Wash beans and put in large stockpot. Add water to cover and add salt. Soak overnight. Drain and add remaining ingredients. Simmer over low to medium heat for 3–4 hours or until tender. Remove ham hock. Pick meat off bone and return meat to pot. Discard bone and fat. Soup is ready to serve.

New Orleans Oyster Stew

YIELD: 6 SERVINGS

I call this New Orleans Oyster Stew because it is the way we like it there—the simplest oyster stew in the world.

1   pint shucked oysters
1   pint milk
1   pint heavy cream
2   tablespoons butter
     Salt and freshly ground black pepper to taste

Put the oysters with their liquor in a small pan. Put the milk and cream in another. Heat both until the edges of the oysters begin to curl; then combine the contents of the two pans and stir just to mix. Add butter. As soon as it melts, salt and pepper to taste and serve at once.

Sopa de Ajo con Garbanzos (Garlic Soup with Garbanzos)

YIELD: 6 SERVINGS

- 1½ cups dried garbanzos (chick-peas) (see Note)
- 3 teaspoons chopped garlic
- ½ teaspoon coarse salt
- ½ cup chopped fresh mint
- ¼ cup finely chopped fresh parsley
- ¼ cup olive oil
- 1 quart chicken stock
  Croutons, for garnish
  Mint sprigs, for garnish

Wash dried garbanzos under running water, place in a bowl, cover with cold water, and soak for at least 8 hours or overnight. Drain the garbanzos, place in a heavy saucepan, cover with fresh water, and simmer for about 2 hours or until tender. Add more water to simmering pot from time to time, if necessary Drain. (If using canned garbanzos, simply drain liquid in which they are canned.) Mash garlic, salt, and mint to a paste in a food processor. Add the parsley and slowly add the olive oil, a little at a time, until thoroughly absorbed.

In a large saucepan, bring stock to boil. Reduce heat, add drained garbanzos and simmer until garbanzos are heated through. Add garlic paste. Stir to distribute evenly.

Serve from a tureen or individual soup bowls. Scatter croutons on top and garnish with mint sprigs.

NOTE: Canned garbanzos (about 3 cups) may be substituted, but I find that they do not have the crispness of the dried garbanzos.

Potage Olympus

YIELD: 6 SERVINGS

This dish takes time and work, but it makes a one-meal feast.

4	pounds meaty beef brisket, hacked by the butcher in several places, but not all the way through
2	carrots
1	turnip
1	small head cabbage
6	spears asparagus
2	medium pods okra
1	stalk celery
1	small bunch parsley
1	large potato
1	large onion
1	handful each green beans, peas, lima beans, spinach (or other good greens)
1	24-ounce can tomatoes
1	bay leaf
1	pinch dried thyme
	Salt and freshly ground black pepper to taste
1	cup rice (optional)

Put the brisket in a large pot, cover with cold water, and boil for at least half an hour. Then skim carefully and add all the vegetables, washed and cut up coarsely. Finally, add the can of tomatoes with juice, the bay leaf, and the thyme, the latter rubbed in the palm of your hand to bring out the flavor. Simmer very slowly, for 3–4 hours. Salt and pepper to taste.

A cup of rice may be added, for thickening, about 20 minutes before the soup is done. Serve with Jalapeño Corn Bread (page 142).

Gypsy Stew

YIELD: 10–12 HEFTY SERVINGS

In his travels in Spain with the gypsies, Vicente Romero, the world-famous flamenco dancer, discovered this marvelous gypsy chicken stew. Vicente has improved upon the quality and taste by adding green chiles.

1   3-lb. whole chicken fryer, plus 4–5 extra breast halves
6   yellow onions, peeled and quartered
15   garlic cloves, peeled and halved
1   quart cocktail sherry
1   16-ounce can chicken broth
4½   cups roasted and peeled fresh green chiles (page xiv) *or* 9 4-ounce cans whole green chiles
2   24-ounce cans whole tomatoes
2   teaspoons salt or to taste
1   pound Monterey Jack cheese

NOTE: Never *boil* this stew. Boiling will ruin it because all of the sherry will cook out. On the other hand, if it's not cooked enough, it will taste bitter.

Put chicken, onions, garlic, half the sherry, and the broth into a large, heavy soup pot or Dutch oven. If the liquid isn't enough to cover the other ingredients, add more broth or water. Cover pot and simmer *slowly* for 1–1½ hours or until chicken is cooked.

Cut chiles into chunks. Using 2 forks, tear tomatoes apart and place in large bowl with chiles and all of their juices, to mingle together while chicken is cooking.

Remove cooked chicken and let cool enough so you can pick meat off bones. Add chiles, tomatoes, remaining sherry, salt, and chicken to the soup. Cover and simmer *slowly* for about an hour.

Cut chunks of cheese into cubes and place in bottom of individual serving bowls. Pour stew into each bowl; the heat will melt the cheese. Serve with Flour Tortillas (page 140) and a side dish of guacamole (page 6) or beans.

Green Chile Stew

YIELD: 6 SERVINGS

2	tablespoons olive oil
2	pounds boneless pork, cut into 1-inch cubes
½	cup chopped onion
1	clove garlic, minced
¼	cup flour
2	cups peeled and chopped fresh tomatoes (page xiv)
2	cups roasted, peeled, and chopped fresh green chiles (page xiv) or 2 7-ounce cans green chiles, drained and chopped
1	fresh jalapeño pepper, chopped
1	teaspoon salt
½	teaspoon freshly ground black pepper
½	teaspoon sugar
1	cup chicken or beef broth

Heat olive oil in 4-quart Dutch oven with cover. Add pork and cook until lightly browned. Add onion and garlic and stir with meat. Add flour and stir 1–2 minutes. Add tomatoes, green chiles, jalapeño, salt, pepper, and sugar. Mix to incorporate. Add broth. Lower heat. Cover pot and simmer for 1–1½ hours or until meat is tender. Serve with Flour Tortillas (page 140).

Shrimp and Corn Chowder

YIELD: 6 SERVINGS

Pinot Chardonnay marries well with this chowder.

6 cups chicken stock
3 pounds medium shrimp, shelled and deveined
4 slices bacon
1 tablespoon butter
1 cup chopped celery
¾ cup chopped onion
¾ cup chopped green bell pepper
¾ cup chopped red bell pepper
2 cups fresh corn kernels (scraped from about 4 ears of fresh corn) *or* 1 16-ounce can cream-style corn
1 medium carrot, sliced very thin
2 tablespoons cornstarch
1 cup cold milk
½ teaspoon Tabasco sauce
Salt and freshly ground black pepper to taste
1 cup heavy cream

In a large 3- or 4-quart heavy pot, bring 3 cups of the chicken stock to a boil. Add shrimp and return to a boil for 2 minutes (until shrimp turns pink); *do not overcook.* Remove shrimp with slotted spoon and reserve broth. Reserve 24 shrimp and liquefy remaining shrimp in a blender with the remaining 3 cups of cold chicken stock. In a separate skillet, fry bacon until crisp. Drain on a paper towel and reserve for garnish. Add butter to bacon grease and sauté celery, onion, and peppers for 2–3 minutes.

Add liquefied shrimp to the hot reserved broth. Add corn and carrots. Cook for 2 minutes, stirring constantly. Add sautéed vegetables to shrimp mixture. Dissolve cornstarch in milk and add to mixture. Bring to a boil and cook 2 minutes. Add Tabasco, salt, pepper, and heavy cream and blend together thoroughly. Place 4 shrimp in each of 6 bowls; cover with chowder. Sprinkle with crumbled bacon.

Chicken and Sausage Gumbo

YIELD: 6 SERVINGS

Of the many popular Creole songs, my favorite is "The Rooster and the Chicken"—about the favorite soup of Louisiana. The words are:

> The rooster and the chicken had a fight,
> the chicken knocked the rooster out of sight,
> the rooster told the chicken, "that's all right,
> I'll meet you in the gumbo tomorrow night."

Crisp Chablis will complement this gumbo.

½ cup lard
⅓ cup flour
1 cup chopped onion
¼ cup chopped green bell pepper
1 tablespoon finely chopped fresh parsley
1 clove garlic, minced
1 quart chicken broth
½ pound smoked sausage, sliced thin
¼ pound smoked ham, cut into ½-inch slices
2½–3 pounds chicken breasts, poached (page 82) and shredded
1 teaspoon salt
¼ teaspoon cayenne pepper
½ teaspoon dried oregano
½ teaspoon dried thyme
2 tablespoons filé powder (see Note)
3 cups boiled rice

NOTE: Filé powder can be found in supermarkets or specialty stores.

First prepare roux: Heat lard in a heavy 10-inch skillet. When smoking, add flour and *stir constantly* until roux is golden brown and completely dry. This may take as long as 20–30 minutes and requires constant stirring to prevent burning.

Add onion, green pepper, parsley, and garlic. Work into roux until smoothly distributed. Put 1 pint of the chicken broth in a large 3- to 4-quart pot and add roux, mixing well. Add sausage and ham and cook 10 minutes over low to moderate heat. Add remaining broth, shredded chicken and seasonings, except for filé powder. Bring to a boil. Reduce heat and simmer for 1 hour. Remove from heat. Add filé powder until gumbo strings from the spoon. Serve over boiled rice in deep soup bowls.

Halibut, Corn, and Green Chile Chowder

YIELD: 6 SERVINGS

2 pounds fresh halibut fillets
4 slices bacon, diced
¾ cup chopped onions
2 cups diced Idaho potatoes
1½ cups clam broth
1½ teaspoons salt
¼ teaspoon freshly ground black pepper
¼ teaspoon dried dill weed
2 cups fresh corn kernels (scraped from about 4 ears) or 1 16-ounce can cream-style corn
1¼ cups roasted and peeled fresh green chiles, cut into strips, or 1 10-ounce can whole green chiles, cut into strips
4 cups half-and-half
1½ tablespoons butter
1½ tablespoons flour
1 tablespoon chopped fresh parsley, for garnish

Remove skin from halibut and cut into 1-inch cubes. In a heavy 3- or 4-quart soup kettle, cook bacon until crisp. Add onions and sauté until limp. Add potatoes, clam broth, salt, pepper, and dill weed. Cover and simmer for 15 minutes. Add fish and simmer until fish flakes easily (about 6–7 minutes; test with a fork). Add corn and green chiles, then the half-and-half, and heat slowly. Make a paste with the butter and flour, then add to the chowder, stirring constantly until thickened. Serve very hot. Garnish with chopped parsley.

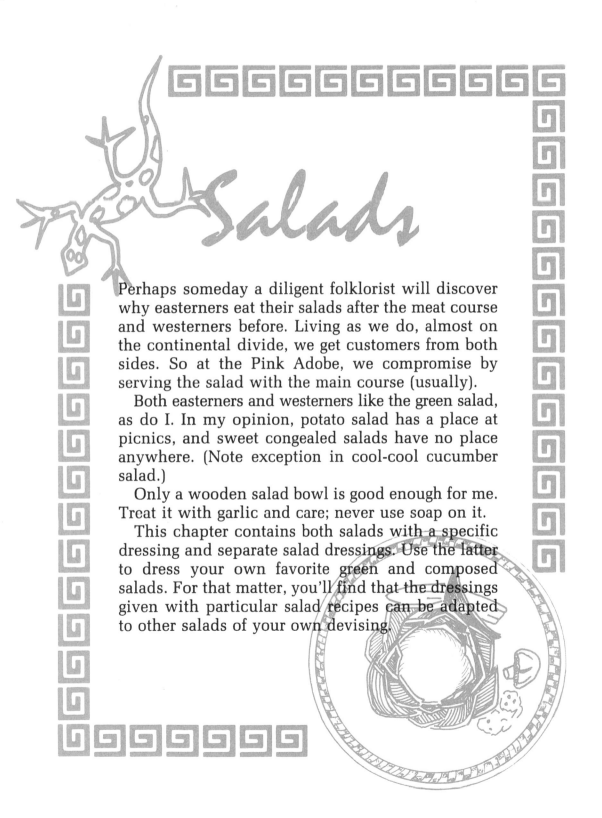

Salads

Perhaps someday a diligent folklorist will discover why easterners eat their salads after the meat course and westerners before. Living as we do, almost on the continental divide, we get customers from both sides. So at the Pink Adobe, we compromise by serving the salad with the main course (usually).

Both easterners and westerners like the green salad, as do I. In my opinion, potato salad has a place at picnics, and sweet congealed salads have no place anywhere. (Note exception in cool-cool cucumber salad.)

Only a wooden salad bowl is good enough for me. Treat it with garlic and care; never use soap on it.

This chapter contains both salads with a specific dressing and separate salad dressings. Use the latter to dress your own favorite green and composed salads. For that matter, you'll find that the dressings given with particular salad recipes can be adapted to other salads of your own devising.

Avocado Halves Stuffed with Chicken in Chile Sauce

YIELD: 6 SERVINGS

This makes a very tempting luncheon dish. The dressing is a variation on the Pink Adobe Seafood Dressing (page 49).

Chile Sauce Dressing

1	cup mayonnaise (page 54)
1	cup bottled chile sauce
1	teaspoon capers
1	teaspoon chili powder
1	teaspoon chopped pickled jalapeño pepper (or to taste)
¼	teaspoon salt
¼	teaspoon crushed fresh cilantro

Salad

3	cups cooked chicken, cut into ½-inch cubes
6	large romaine lettuce leaves
3	ripe avocados, halved, pitted, and peeled
1	medium tomato, peeled and cut into wedges
2	hard-cooked eggs, cut into wedges
12	black olives, pitted
2	tablespoons minced fresh chives

Prepare dressing: Mix all dressing ingredients together in a large bowl with a rubber spatula. Set aside.

In another bowl, add dressing a little at a time to cubed chicken using just enough to moisten. Be sure mixture is firm enough to mound into avocado halves. Place a leaf of lettuce on individual plates. Place an avocado half on each plate and divide chicken mixture evenly among avocados. Garnish plates with tomato, eggs, and olives. Sprinkle tops with chives. Serve remaining dressing separately. Serve with buttered hot Flour Tortillas (see page 140).

Bibb Lettuce with Grilled Brie Toast

YIELD: 6 SERVINGS

This salad is simple elegance. Prepared with the best lettuce and Brie ripened to perfection and served on your loveliest platter, it makes an impressive presentation for an important dinner party.

1	head Bibb lettuce
½	cup Basic French Dressing (page 53)
1	loaf French bread
6	tablespoons unsalted butter, softened
¼	cup Dijon mustard
1	pound Brie sliced thin vertically

Preheat broiler. Remove lettuce leaves from core. Wash and dry leaves thoroughly. Place in center of large platter and cover with dressing. Slice bread into ¾-inch strips. Spread with butter, then mustard. Cover with sliced Brie. Arrange strips on a baking sheet and place under broiler until cheese begins to bubble. Arrange bread strips on a platter around Bibb lettuce.

Cool-Cool Cucumber Salad

YIELD: 6 SERVINGS

1	envelope (1 tablespoon) lime gelatin
1	cup boiling water
1	tablespoon white wine vinegar
1	cup mayonnaise (page 54)
1	cup grated and drained cucumber
1	tablespoon grated onion
1	tablespoon prepared hot horseradish
¼	teaspoon salt

Dissolve the gelatin in boiling water. Add the vinegar, stir, and chill until slightly thickened. Fold in the other ingredients. Pour into 1 one-quart or 6 individual molds. Chill until firm.

Pink Adobe Famous Chicken Salad

YIELD: 6–8 SERVINGS

This is the most popular salad on our summer menu. It is a marvelous dish to serve year-round, either in individual servings for a luncheon or on one large platter for a buffet.

Chicken

2	2½- to 3-pound frying chickens
	Salt to taste
1	carrot
1	small onion
2	sprigs parsley
½	teaspoon freshly ground black pepper

Marinade

- 1   cup extra-virgin olive oil
- ½   cup finely chopped scallions
- ½   cup finely chopped fresh parsley

Salad

- 2   cups diced celery
- 1   cup walnut pieces
     Salt and freshly ground black pepper to taste
- 1   head romaine or other lettuce
- 2   cups mayonnaise (page 54)
     Pimiento-stuffed green olives, chopped or sliced black olives, chopped hard-cooked eggs, chopped fresh parsley, for garnish

Place chickens in large pot, salt slightly, and cover with water. Add carrot, onion, parsley, and pepper. Bring to a boil and cook until tender (approximately 1 hour). Remove chickens from pot and let cool. Remove meat and discard skin and bones, keeping breasts in one piece.

While chicken is cooking, prepare marinade: Combine marinade ingredients in a mixing bowl. Divide marinade into two flat containers. When cool, slice chicken breast meat thin and place in one container of marinade. Chop rest of chicken into small pieces and place in the other container of marinade. Refrigerate both for several hours or overnight.

When ready to assemble salad, remove chopped chicken from marinade. Place in large bowl with celery, walnuts, and salt and pepper to taste. Mix gently. Place romaine strips or chopped lettuce on 6 individual plates or one large platter. Mound chicken mixture on each plate or shape onto one platter. Cover completely with thin slices of chicken breast. With rubber spatula, spread entire mound with mayonnaise. Decorate with garnishes as desired.

NOTE: For a decorating suggestion, my version is featured on this book's cover.

Many Bean Salad

This salad can be made with as many of a variety of beans as you desire, though I find the dish loses color without black beans. Many specialty food shops carry packages of mixed dry beans, with up to seven different varieties.

Using dry beans takes time: soaking overnight and then two to three hours of cooking, with occasional stirring. You can reduce cooking time to less than one hour, without soaking, by using a pressure cooker. If you're really pressed for time, use canned beans.

Dressing

2	tablespoons mild cider vinegar
½	teaspoon sugar
¼	teaspoon salt
⅛	teaspoon freshly ground black pepper
½	teaspoon Dijon mustard
5	tablespoons olive oil

Salad

1	cup each cooked dry or canned and drained pinto beans, black beans, garbanzo beans, cut green beans, and white beans
¼	cup chopped green bell pepper
1	cup thinly sliced red onion
1	medium tomato, chopped
½	cup mayonnaise (page 54)

Prepare dressing by mixing together all dressing ingredients except the oil. A screwtop jar is ideal for this. Mix in olive oil and shake well. In a large bowl, combine beans, bell pepper, and onion using a rubber spatula to avoid breaking the beans. Pour dressing over the salad and mix gently. Just before serving, stir in tomatoes and mayonnaise.

Ensalada Duquesa de Argyll

YIELD: 6 SERVINGS

This salad was created for a private party held at the Pink in honor of the Duchess of Argyll. For this party the salads were individually made and served as a separate course after the main entree; however, for a summer buffet or family dinner, use a tray or large platter and on it make one big, bountiful salad using the ingredients in the order named.

1   head romaine lettuce
1   head butter lettuce
1   head endive
1   bunch watercress
½   teaspoon dried salad herbs (Spice Island brand makes an excellent blend of salad herbs)
1   fresh pineapple, peeled, cored, and cut into spears
1   purple onion (Spanish onion), sliced thin
2–3 avocados, peeled and sliced lengthwise about 1 inch thick
1   small bunch white seedless grapes
     About 1 cup Basic French Dressing (page 53)
     Watercress sprigs, for garnish
⅓   cup chopped fresh parsley, for garnish

Place one romaine leaf on each of 6 plates. Break other greens by hand and place on top of each leaf. Reserve a few sprigs of watercress for garnish. Sprinkle greens with salad herbs. Next, place 3–4 pineapple spears on each plate and cover with several slices of onion. Then place a few slices of avocado over the onion and on the avocado place some chopped and whole grapes. Moisten with French dressing, then garnish with watercress and parsley.

Farmers' Market Garden Salad

YIELD: 6 SERVINGS

A perfect mid-summer salad, when locally grown vegetables are available. At most farmers' markets, they are brought in every Saturday morning, freshly picked only hours before.

3   medium tomatoes
4   large ears corn
½   cup chopped fresh green chiles
1   clove garlic, minced
1   tablespoon crushed fresh cilantro

Dressing

2   tablespoons mild vinegar
¼   teaspoon sugar
¼   teaspoon salt
⅛   teaspoon freshly ground black pepper
½   teaspoon Dijon mustard
5   tablespoons olive oil

Drop tomatoes into 4 quarts boiling water for 1 minute. Then peel; skin should slip off easily. Place tomatoes in a bowl of ice water to cool and then chop coarse. Drop shucked corn into boiling water and boil for 3–4 minutes; *do not overcook.* Drain and cool. Scrape kernels from cob with a sharp knife. In a large wooden salad bowl combine the chopped tomatoes, corn, green chiles, garlic, and cilantro. Toss to mix.

Prepare dressing in a screwtop jar: Shake vinegar with sugar, salt, pepper, and mustard, until salt and sugar are dissolved. Add olive oil and shake until well mixed. Pour over salad in bowl. Mix gently.

Old South Salad

YIELD: 6 SERVINGS

This is really tops if the vegetables are freshly picked from the garden. In the South, we eat it with corn on the cob and black-eyed peas, and these should be freshly picked, too. This is guaranteed to bring tears of nostalgia to any old southern eyes.

1   cucumber, peeled and sliced paper-thin
1   medium ripe tomato, sliced paper-thin
1   white onion, sliced paper-thin
1   teaspoon sugar
     Salt and freshly ground black pepper to taste
1   cup vinegar

Place vegetables in a bowl in layers, sprinkling sugar, salt, and pepper on each layer. Cover with the vinegar, using more if necessary. Let stand for about an hour.

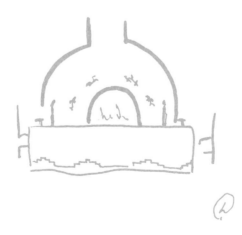

Lobster Salad

NOTE: At the Pink Adobe we use the African rock lobster tails because we're a long way from salt water, and they are very good. You may, of course, substitute whole live lobster, but you will probably need 2–3 pounds because there is more waste on a whole lobster than on lobster tails. Cook as for the lobster tails.

YIELD: 4 SERVINGS

This is a whole meal for a hot day, and a wonderful one at that. It should be served on a large platter to give it the appearance of luxury that it deserves. A perennial favorite at the Pink Adobe.

Lobster

1	onion quartered (unpeeled)
½	lemon
1	bay leaf
6	whole cloves
¼	teaspoon pickling spice
¼	teaspoon cayenne pepper
	Salt and freshly ground black pepper to taste
2	1-pound frozen lobster tails (uncooked) (see Note)

Salad

½	head each leaf and iceberg lettuce
4	stalks heart celery, chopped
1	bell pepper, chopped
1	cup grated cheddar cheese
1	cup cooked and chilled green beans
½	cup chopped fresh parsley
10	pitted black olives
2	large fresh tomatoes, cut into wedges, for garnish
3	hard-cooked eggs, cut into wedges, for garnish

Pink Adobe Seafood Dressing

    1   cup mayonnaise (page 54)
    1   cup bottled chile sauce
    1   teaspoon capers
    1   pinch dried basil
    1   pinch dried tarragon
    1   pinch dried savory

Place onion, lemon, bay leaf, cloves, pickling spice, cayenne, and salt and pepper to taste in enough water to be able to cover the lobster tails. Bring to a boil. Drop lobster in and boil for 20 minutes. Remove the lobster and take the meat out of the shells. Chill in refrigerator.

While the lobster meat is chilling, prepare the dressing: Mix all dressing ingredients together, being sure to first rub the herbs in the palm of your hands to bring out their flavor.

Assemble the salad: Arrange the outer crisp leaves of lettuce on a very large platter. Break the heart of the lettuce and arrange in a loose mound in the center. Cover entire plate with celery, green pepper, cheddar cheese, and green beans. Cut the lobster meat into chunks and place on top of this mound. Cover generously with the seafood dressing. Sprinkle the salad with parsley and place the olives judiciously on the mound. Garnish the edge of the platter with tomato and egg wedges.

Potato Salad with Green Chiles

YIELD: 4 SERVINGS

2	pounds Idaho potatoes
4	fresh green chiles, roasted and peeled, *or* 1 4-ounce can whole green chiles
½	teaspoon sugar
2	tablespoons cider vinegar
2	tablespoons olive oil
1	teaspoon salt
½	teaspoon freshly ground black pepper
½	cup finely chopped onion
1	teaspoon prepared mustard
1½	cups mayonnaise (page 54)
1	cup crumbled goat cheese

In salted water to cover, boil potatoes with skins on until tender, about 30 minutes; *do not overcook*. When cool, peel potatoes and cut into ½-inch cubes. Cut chiles into 1½-inch strips. Combine chiles and potatoes. Gently toss with sugar, vinegar, and olive oil. Add salt, pepper, and onion. Mix mustard with mayonnaise and fold into potato mixture. Toss gently but thoroughly. Turn into serving bowl and sprinkle top with cheese.

Turkey and Kidney Bean Salad

YIELD: 6 SERVINGS

1	head romaine lettuce
1	head leaf lettuce, shredded
2	cups Spicy Spanish Dressing (double following recipe)
1	15¼-ounce can dark red kidney beans
1	cup sliced black olives
2	cups shredded cooked turkey
1	avocado
1	tablespoon fresh lemon juice
1	tablespoon chopped pickled jalapeño pepper
½	cup dairy sour cream
½	cup grated cheddar cheese
1	pound tortilla chips, for garnish

Line each of 6 individual salad plates with a leaf of romaine lettuce. Break up remaining romaine and mix with shredded leaf lettuce. Place on top of plates. Divide dressing in half and reserve one-half to serve at the table.

Using the other half: spoon 1 tablespoon of dressing over each plate. Toss kidney beans and olives with half of the remaining dressing (5 tablespoons) and divide among the 6 plates. Mix turkey with remaining dressing (5 tablespoons) and place on top of bean mixture.

Mash avocado with lemon juice and jalapeño and place on top of each serving of turkey. Top each with a dollop of sour cream and sprinkle with grated cheese. Garnish each plate with tortilla chips. Pass the reserved salad dressing separately at the table.

Salad Dressings

Spicy Spanish Dressing

YIELD: 1 CUP

3	tablespoons cider vinegar
¼	teaspoon salt
1	teaspoon sugar
¼	teaspoon dried oregano
¼	teaspoon ground cumin
1	clove garlic, minced
½	teaspoon Tabasco sauce
¾	cup olive oil

In blender, mix all ingredients except oil. When well combined, add oil and blend for 1 minute.

Creamy Fruit Salad Dressing

YIELD: 1½ CUPS

1	cup sliced ripe strawberries
2	tablespoons honey
1	tablespoon orange juice
½	cup mayonnaise (page 54)

Place all ingredients in a food processor. With on/off movement process for a few seconds. The strawberries should *not* be mashed completely. Pour over fresh fruits of your choice.

Basic French Dressing

YIELD: 2 CUPS

½ cup balsamic or red wine vinegar
2 drops garlic juice (use a garlic press)
1 teaspoon salt
½ teaspoon freshly ground black pepper
¼ teaspoon sugar
1½ cups olive oil

Put all ingredients except the olive oil in a screwtop jar. Shake to blend well. Add olive oil and shake to blend. This dressing keeps well in the refrigerator. Shake well each time before using.

Variations

Dijon Dressing: Add 1 teaspoon Dijon mustard.

Herb Dressing: Experiment carefully with any combination of fresh or dried tarragon, basil, thyme, marjoram, savory, cilantro. Be cautious. Add herbs only until the flavor becomes tantalizing, not overpowering. Always rub dried herbs in your palms before adding to the dressing.

Roquefort Dressing: Process 1 cup Roquefort cheese in a food processor until smooth, then slowly pour the French dressing through the feed tube until blended. Yields approximately 3 cups.

Blender Mayonnaise

YIELD: ABOUT 1½ CUPS

I find that blender mayonnaise is superior to that made in a food processor. Though you may use a good-quality bottled mayonnaise in any of the recipes that call for it, there is nothing like homemade mayonnaise.

- 1 egg
- 1 teaspoon dry mustard
- 1 teaspoon salt
- ⅛ teaspoon cayenne pepper
- 1¼ cups oil, half vegetable and half olive oil (½ cup plus 1 tablespoon each)
- 3 tablespoons fresh lemon juice

Blend egg with mustard, salt, cayenne, and ¼ cup of the oil until combined. Add lemon juice and slowly add remaining oil. Blend; mixture should be thick. It may be necessary to stop the blender during processing and scrape down sides.

Green Mayonnaise

YIELD: 3 CUPS

Green mayonnaise is good with fish, on hamburgers, and as a dip for vegetables.

- 1 cup fresh spinach, washed, stems and ribs removed
- ½ cup chopped fresh parsley, stems removed
- ½ cup chopped chives or scallions
- 2 tablespoons capers
- 1½ cups mayonnaise (recipe above)

In food processor with a steel blade, process spinach, parsley, chives, and capers to a paste. In large bowl, fold spinach paste into mayonnaise with a rubber spatula until well blended.

Ricotta Dill Dressing

YIELD: 2 CUPS

This dressing is best when used to make potato salad, but it can also be used as a dip for raw vegetables or to dress a salad of other cooked vegetables.

1   cup ricotta cheese
1   cup buttermilk
¼   cup chopped onion
1   tablespoon chopped fresh parsley
2   tablespoons chopped fresh dill
⅛   teaspoon dry mustard

Mix all ingredients in blender until combined, but do not overmix.

Seafood

The versatility of seafood is truly impressive. Whether it is the wondrous food of the sea or gulf or a tender fish from the freshwater lakes, a cook with a gentle way can transform it into a dish of savory goodness and tantalizing flavors.

Though Santa Fe is not near the sea, at the Pink Adobe we serve a variety of seafood dishes, including several shellfish entrees and salads. I've found that frozen African rock lobster tails are a fine substitute for live lobsters, but you should always opt for fresh fish and shellfish as available. Again, feel free to substitute one type for another as appropriate.

Stuffed Crabs Cajun Style

YIELD: 6 SERVINGS

This is not the Creole cookery of New Orleans, but the Cajun of the bayou country. In the 200 years that these people of Breton and Norman blood have been in Louisiana, they have taken over the shrimping, crabbing, and oyster-tonging industry. They are also fine hunters, trappers, and, of course, cooks.

6	hard-shelled crabs or 3 cups thawed frozen crabmeat
1	teaspoon minced onion
1½	tablespoons butter
2	tablespoons flour
½	cup milk
1	egg yolk
½	teaspoon prepared horseradish
4	tablespoons chopped fresh parsley
½	teaspoon salt
½	teaspoon prepared mustard
1	dash cayenne pepper
4	drops Tabasco sauce
1	tablespoon fresh lemon juice
½	teaspoon Worcestershire sauce
½	cup buttered bread crumbs

Preheat oven to 350°F. In a pot of boiling salted water, drop in the 6 crabs and cook for 20 minutes. Drain, cool, break off claws, and pick out solid meat from the claws and crab body, discarding all spongy parts. Scrub large upper shells and set aside. (If using thawed frozen crabmeat, no cooking is required; pick through crabmeat carefully to remove any shell and cartilage.)

In a medium skillet, brown onion in butter. Blend in flour, add milk, and stir until thickened. Add egg yolk, horseradish, 2 tablespoons of the parsley, the salt, mustard, cayenne pepper, and Tabasco. Remove from heat. Stir in the crabmeat, lemon juice, Worcestershire sauce, and half the bread crumbs. Fill each shell with this mixture and top with remaining bread crumbs and parsley. (If using frozen crabmeat, stuff mixture into other shells or individual shallow baking dishes.) Bake until brown, about 15 minutes.

Baked Red Snapper with Green Chile

YIELD: 6 SERVINGS

6   fresh red snapper fillets (to total about 2 pounds)

Sauce

2   tablespoons olive oil
½   cup chopped onion
¼   cup chopped celery
1   teaspoon fresh chopped jalapeño pepper
½   cup peeled and chopped fresh tomato
1   clove garlic, minced
1   pound roasted, peeled and chopped fresh green chile
     or 1 can (15 ounces) chopped green chile
½   cup Madeira wine
½   teaspoon salt
⅛   teaspoon pepper
1   teaspoon fresh chopped cilantro or 1 teaspoon dried
     coriander
     Additional salt and pepper to taste
1   tablespoon lemon juice

In saucepan combine olive oil, onion, celery, chopped jalapeño, tomato, and garlic. Cover and cook until tender (about 5 minutes.) Stir in green chile, Madeira wine, salt, pepper, and cilantro. Bring to a boil and simmer for 10 minutes. Using an 8-by-12-by-2-inch baking dish, ladle ½ cup cooked chile sauce on bottom of dish. Place fish portions on sauce in baking dish. Sprinkle with salt and pepper to taste, and lemon juice. Pour remaining sauce over fish. Bake in 350° oven, uncovered, for 15 to 20 minutes or until fish flakes easily when tested with a fork.

Hot Crabmeat Sandwich

YIELD: 2 SERVINGS

1   cup fresh or frozen flaked crabmeat
1   clove garlic, minced
1   tablespoon olive oil
1   egg
1   tablespoon cream
    Dash salt
    Dash cayenne pepper
    Dash Tabasco sauce
2   hot buttered buns

Pick the crabmeat over carefully to remove the shell and cartilage. Sauté garlic in olive oil. Add the crabmeat and mix well. Keep warm. In mixing bowl, beat the egg gently and stir in the cream, salt, cayenne, and Tabasco. Stir this very slowly and very gently into the hot crabmeat and cook over low heat. Do not stop the gentle stirring until the mixture is light and the egg has set. Spread on buttered, toasted buns at once.

Fish Diablo

YIELD: 6 SERVINGS

Louis Jadot Macon Blanc—Villages is an excellent wine choice with this fish.

6   fresh fillets of sole or flounder (about 1½ pounds total)
    Juice of 1–2 limes (to taste)

Sauce

2   tablespoons butter
¼   cup chopped onion
1   clove garlic, chopped
2   teaspoons diced jalapeño pepper
2   teaspoons chopped black olives
1   cup Salsa Diabolique (page 22) or 1 7-ounce can green chile salsa
1   tablespoon dry sherry
½   teaspoon dried oregano

Lime wedges, for garnish
Chopped cilantro, for garnish

Preheat the oven to 350°F. Arrange fish in a 9-by-12-by-2-inch baking dish. Sprinkle liberally with lime juice. Cover dish with waxed paper and set aside.

Prepare sauce: Combine butter, onion, garlic, jalapeño, olives, salsa, sherry, and oregano in a 2-quart saucepan. Bring to a simmer and allow to simmer for 5 minutes. Pour sauce over fish and bake, uncovered, for 30 minutes or until fish flakes. Garnish with lime wedges and chopped cilantro.

Avocado Dream Boats

YIELD: 6 SERVINGS

Some time ago, I was invited by the California Avocado Advisory Board to participate in a contest they were sponsoring—for chefs only. While I did not win the top prize of a trip to Europe, I was proud to receive the silver medal for this recipe.

3   large, firmly ripe avocados
1   lime
1   6-ounce package green noodles

Sauce

4   tablespoons butter
4   tablespoons flour
4–5 dashes Tabasco sauce
½   teaspoon salt
1   cup heavy cream
1   cup milk
¾   cup grated cheddar cheese

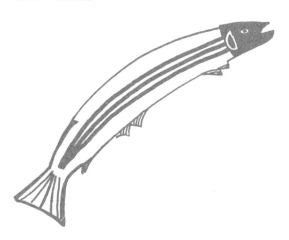

Filling

1½	cups mayonnaise (page 54)
2	teaspoons Dijon mustard
2	teaspoons French's prepared mustard
1	medium bell pepper, chopped fine
1	teaspoon salt
¼	teaspoon white pepper
2	pimientos, chopped
2	large eggs, beaten
1	cup coarsely broken cooked lobster meat
1	cup coarsely broken cooked shrimp
1	cup coarsely broken lump crabmeat

Topping

6	additional dollops mayonnaise
	Paprika, for garnish
¼	cup chopped fresh parsley, for garnish

Preheat oven to 350°F. Halve and peel the avocados. Remove pits. Drizzle with juice from the lime and set in refrigerator. Cook the noodles according to package directions. Drain and set aside in a colander.

Prepare sauce: Melt butter in a large, heavy skillet over low heat. Gradually add flour, stirring constantly. Add Tabasco and salt. When mixture is bubbly, combine cream and milk and add slowly, stirring constantly until it begins to thicken. Add cheese and stir until it is melted.

If noodles are stuck together, run cold water over them to separate. Mix noodles with sauce and place in a 9-by-12-by-2-inch casserole dish. Arrange avocado halves on top of noodles.

Prepare filling: Combine mayonnaise, mustards, bell pepper, salt, white pepper, pimientos, and eggs. Very gently, fold in seafood. Be careful not to break the pieces. Generously spoon this mixture into each avocado half.

Top each with a dollop of mayonnaise. Bake for 25 minutes or until puffy. Garnish with paprika and chopped parsley.

Lobster Club Sandwich on Pita Bread

YIELD: 6 SERVINGS

6	teaspoons butter, softened
6	pita bread pockets, 1 inch of top sliced off each
12	ounces cooked lobster meat
12	slices bacon, fried crisp and drained on paper towel
6	lettuce leaves, shredded
1	cup peeled and chopped fresh tomato
6	tablespoons mayonnaise (page 54)
6	black olives, pitted
6	baby sweet gherkins

Preheat oven to 350°F. Spread butter inside each pocket and place pitas on cookie sheet. Heat in oven for 3–4 minutes. Open pockets, being careful not to split sides. Place 2 ounces of lobster meat into each pocket, followed by 2 slices of bacon, lettuce, and tomatoes, evenly divided. Top tomatoes in each sandwich with 1 tablespoon of mayonnaise. Spear an olive and a gherkin on a frilled toothpick. Place on top of each sandwich.

Deviled Lobster Tails

YIELD: 6 SERVINGS

Serve these lobster tails with a bottle of Trimbach Alsace Riesling.

1   tablespoon salt
1   teaspoon cayenne pepper
10 whole cloves
½   lemon
1   small onion, sliced
1   teaspoon peppercorns
4   8-ounce fresh or frozen lobster tails
½   cup chopped celery
½   cup chopped onion
½   cup chopped green bell pepper
¼   cup chopped fresh parsley
4   tablespoons butter
2   hard-cooked eggs, chopped
1   raw egg
6   drops Tabasco sauce
2   cups buttered bread crumbs
    Salt and freshly ground black pepper to taste
    Milk
6   demitasses of melted butter (see Note)

Preheat oven to 350°F. Put 1 tablespoon salt, the cayenne pepper, cloves, lemon, sliced onion, and peppercorns in a large pot of water and bring to a boil. Drop in lobster tails. Keep at a full rolling boil for 20 minutes. Take out the lobster tails, split in half lengthwise, and remove the meat. Save 6 half shells.

Sauté the chopped celery, onion, green bell pepper, and parsley in the butter until the onion is transparent. Break lobster meat into chunks in a large bowl. Gently stir in the sautéed vegetables, hard-cooked eggs, raw egg, Tabasco, 1 cup of the bread crumbs, salt and pepper to taste, and just enough milk to make the mixture hold together. Pile the mixture high in each of the 6 half shells and top with the rest of the bread crumbs. Bake until brown, about 20 minutes. Serve at once with a demitasse of melted butter for each portion. Dip each bite in butter when eating.

NOTE: *A demitasse holds about 4 ounces, but you need not offer that much butter per serving. Fill each demitasse or other small dish as desired.*

Oyster and Green Pea Soufflé

YIELD: 6 SERVINGS

2 tablespoons butter
2 tablespoons flour
½ cup milk
1 pint shucked oysters, chopped
4 eggs, separated
1 teaspoon salt
½ teaspoon Worcestershire sauce
  Dash Tabasco sauce
  Dash freshly ground black pepper
2 cups cooked peas

Preheat oven to 350°F. In large heavy skillet, melt butter. Add flour to make a white paste. Add the milk and half the oysters. Bring to a boil, stirring constantly. Remove from heat. Add the egg yolks, one at a time, beating well as each yolk is added. Add the rest of the oysters and the seasonings. Beat the egg whites stiff and fold in. Place the peas in a well-buttered 8-by-10-by-2-inch casserole dish. Pour the oyster mixture over all and bake until browned and fluffy, about 30 minutes.

Oysters Rockefeller

YIELD: 6 SERVINGS

This classic dish hails from faraway New Orleans, but it is dear to my heart and to the hearts of Pink Adobe patrons. It is usually served as an appetizer, but at the Pink Adobe we offer it as an entree. For the wine, try Preuses Chablis Premier Cru.

It is impossible to make this dish in the original manner, since one of the necessary ingredients was absinthe, which is now banned, even in France. Pernod, which has the licorice flavor of absinthe, is a good substitute.

2   cups cooked spinach
3–4 shallots (see note below)
1   bay leaf
4   sprigs parsley
½   teaspoon celery salt
½   teaspoon salt
6   drops Tabasco sauce
5   tablespoons Pernod
½   pound butter
3   dozen oysters in their shells
    Rock salt (see note below)
½   cup bread crumbs

Preheat oven to 400°F. Process the spinach, shallots, bay leaf, and parsley in a food processor until the mixture is very smooth. Add the celery salt, salt, Tabasco, and 3 tablespoons of the Pernod. Melt the butter in a 2-quart saucepan, add the mixed ingredients, and simmer for 5 minutes. While this is cooking, shuck and drain the oysters and replace them in the deep bottom halves of the shells. (If sauce is done before you need it for the next step, keep warm in low-temperature oven.) Pack 6 pie tins with rock salt. Bed the oysters down in the salt. Distribute the rest of the Pernod over the oysters. Mix the bread crumbs into the sauce and cover the oysters with it. Bake for 10 minutes. Serve in the pie tins.

NOTE: *Shallots are small, delicate members of the onion family. Small white onions are a substitute but are a little stronger; the white bulbs of green onions are another alternative but a little milder.*

The purpose of the rock salt is to hold the heat. The dish will be more effective, artistically, if served in a fairly dim light; the salt glows red and adds glamour. Nowadays, rock salt is also called ice cream salt *or* melting salt.

Oysters St. Jacques

YIELD: 6 SERVINGS

This is a famous New Orleans dish and quite a simple one. A bottle of Meursault goes nicely with it.

1	pint shucked oysters
1	tablespoon minced onion
1	tablespoon minced bell pepper
1	tablespoon butter
2	tablespoons flour
1	dash dried thyme
1	bay leaf
	Salt and freshly ground black pepper to taste
1	tablespoon chopped fresh parsley
2	hard-cooked eggs, chopped
1	teaspoon Worcestershire sauce
¼	cup milk
1	cup buttered bread crumbs

Preheat oven to 350°F. Drain oyster liquor into a large pot. Set oysters aside and heat the liquor. While it is heating, sauté the onion and bell pepper in the butter in a heavy skillet until onion is transparent. Add flour to thicken. When thoroughly dry, dilute at once with warm oyster liquor, stirring until smooth. Add thyme, bay leaf, and salt and pepper to taste, remembering that oysters are salty too. Add the oysters, stir well, and simmer for 5–6 minutes. Remove bay leaf and add parsley, eggs, and Worcestershire. Stir and divide into 6 prewarmed ramekins. Cover with bread crumbs and bake until browned, about 15 minutes.

Linguine with Oysters and Green Chiles

YIELD: 6 SERVINGS

For oyster lovers, this is the apex of all pasta dishes.

- 1 quart shucked oysters, with their liquor
- ¼ pound (1 stick) butter
- ¼ cup flour
- 1 cup chopped green onions
- ½ cup minced fresh parsley
- 1 cup roasted, peeled, and chopped fresh green chiles (page xiv)
- 1 tablespoon Worcestershire sauce
  Salt and freshly ground black pepper to taste
- 1 pound linguine noodles
- 6 cups boiling water
  Grated Parmesan cheese (optional)

Drain liquor from oysters into a 1-quart measuring cup. Add enough water to liquor to measure 1 quart. Transfer to medium saucepan. Bring liquid to a simmer and add oysters. Cook for 2–3 minutes, until edges begin to curl. *Do not overcook*, or oysters will be rubbery. Remove oysters and place on a dish. Cover with a buttered sheet of waxed paper. Reserve broth.

In a heavy saucepan, melt butter. When melted, add flour and cook roux, stirring, for 3 minutes. Remove from heat and add the oyster broth in a steady stream. Cook over medium heat for 10 minutes. Reduce heat and add green onions, parsley, green chiles, Worcestershire sauce, and salt and pepper. Simmer for 15 minutes. While sauce is simmering, cook linguine in 6 cups of boiling water to al dente stage. Drain well. Add oysters to sauce and heat for 1 minute. On large plate, pour sauce over cooked linguine. Toss gently and serve. If desired, serve with grated Parmesan cheese.

Pescado Posole

In the Southwest, green corn steamed and dried on the cob, then shelled, is called *chicos*. These are packaged and labeled *posole*. Since packaged or frozen posole may not be available in your area, you will find that canned hominy is easily substituted. The following recipe is the southwestern answer to the French bouillabaisse. Georges DeBoeuf Pouilly Fuisse '85 is a good wine choice.

6	strips bacon
2	cloves garlic, peeled and minced
1	medium onion, chopped coarse
1	tablespoon chili powder
1	teaspoon dried oregano
1	teaspoon sugar
1	teaspoon salt
⅓	cup fresh lime juice
1	jalapeño pepper, chopped
2	29-ounce cans hominy, drained
1	quart chicken stock or clam juice
1	pound medium raw shrimp, peeled and deveined
1	pound firm white fish (such as cod, haddock, or halibut), skinned, boned, and cut into 1-inch pieces
	Accompaniments: Salsa Diabolique (p. 22); chopped red onions; chopped radishes; peeled, seeded, and chopped tomatoes, lime wedges; chopped fresh cilantro; sliced avocado; pitted and chopped black olives

In a large stockpot, fry bacon until crisp. Remove bacon, crumble, and reserve. Drain all but about 2 tablespoons of drippings from pot. To the remaining drippings add the cooked bacon, garlic, onion, chili powder, oregano, sugar, salt, lime juice, jalapeño pepper, and hominy. Add stock to pot and bring to a boil, then reduce heat, cover, and simmer for 15 minutes. Add seafood, cover, and simmer for 5 minutes more, until seafood is cooked through. Taste for seasoning, adding more salt if necessary. Serve in large soup bowls. Have bowls of accompaniments on table to garnish each bowl according to the taste of individual diners. Serve with hot Flour Tortillas (page 140) and Pink Adobe Guacamole (see page 6).

Shrimp Creole

YIELD: 6 SERVINGS

Lytton Springs Zinfandel has the character to stand up to Creole dishes like this one.

1	large onion, sliced
3	stalks celery, chopped
3	tablespoons olive oil
1	tablespoon mild chili powder
2	tablespoons flour
1	17-ounce can tomatoes
1	cup cooked green peas
2	teaspoons sugar
7	drops Tabasco sauce
	Salt to taste
1	cup white wine
1	pound shrimp, shelled, deveined, and cooked
3	cups cooked rice

Sauté onion with celery in olive oil until transparent; mix in chili powder and flour thoroughly. Mix in tomatoes and peas and bring to a simmer. Add sugar, Tabasco, and salt to taste. Add white wine and simmer until thickened, about 15–20 minutes. Add shrimp and cook only until they are heated through. Serve at once on a bed of hot rice.

Scallops Piñon

YIELD: 6 SERVINGS

New Mexico St. Clair Sauvignon Blanc is a perfect complement to these scallops.

1	pound fresh scallops
½	cup bread crumbs
2	tablespoons minced shallots
¼	cup chopped piñons (pine nuts)
1	tablespoon fresh lemon juice
¼	cup dry vermouth
1	tablespoon chopped fresh parsley
½	teaspoon freshly ground black pepper
4	tablespoons butter, melted
¼	cup chopped fresh parsley, for garnish
	Lemon slices, for garnish
	Blender Hollandaise Sauce (page 17)

Preheat oven to 375°F. Combine and gently mix all ingredients except garnishes and Blender Hollandaise Sauce. Divide mixture into 6 scallop shells. Bake for 10–15 minutes until hot and bubbly. Just before serving, garnish with ¼ cup chopped parsley. Serve with lemon slices and Blender Hollandaise Sauce on the side.

Pescado con Salsa Verde

YIELD: 6 SERVINGS

Serve your guests Beltane Ranch Kenwood Chardonnay '84, and you'll have a perfect food-and-wine match.

6   6- to 8-ounce halibut steaks, cut ½ inch thick
     Salt and freshly ground black pepper to taste
½   cup flour

Salsa Verde

⅓   cup olive oil
½   cup minced onion
1   clove garlic, minced
3   tablespoons flour
2   cups clam juice
⅓   cup dry vermouth
1   teaspoon salt
⅓   cup minced fresh parsley
1   cup roasted, peeled, and chopped green chiles (page xiv)
2   tablespoons minced jalapeño or serrano chile pepper
     (optional, depending on the degree of hotness desired)

⅓   cup olive oil
2   tablespoons chopped fresh cilantro, for garnish

Wash halibut and pat dry. Sprinkle with salt and pepper to taste, then dip in flour. Set aside.

Prepare Salsa Verde: In a heavy 2-quart saucepan, heat ⅓ cup olive oil. Add onion and garlic, and sauté until wilted and transparent. Add flour and mix well, then add clam juice and vermouth. Stir constantly with a whisk until sauce boils and thickens slightly. Reduce heat and simmer for about 2 minutes. Add 1 teaspoon salt, the parsley, green chiles, and jalapeño (or serrano) and cook for 1 minute. Keep warm in the top of a double boiler over hot water. In a heavy 12-inch skillet, heat ⅓ cup olive oil over moderate heat. Add fish and cook for 4 minutes on each side, until lightly browned. On each serving plate, mask each fish with Salsa Verde. Garnish with cilantro.

Poached Salmon

YIELD: 6 SERVINGS

Serve this salmon either hot or cold, with the sauce of your choice. I like to use the Russian Cucumber Salad (see page 77). Try a bottle of Batard Montrachet as an accompaniment.

- 2 cups white wine (more or less)
- 1 cup water
- 2 bay leaves
- 2 small whole onions
- 10 peppercorns
- 5–6 pounds salmon

Fill bottom of fish poacher with wine and water. Add bay leaves, onions, and peppercorns. Bring to a boil. Place fish on rack in poacher or wrap in cheesecloth before placing in water so that it does not come apart. Lower heat. Cook for 10–15 minutes. It is done when a knife comes out clean when inserted into salmon.

Rocky Mountain Trout with Crabmeat Mayonnaise

YIELD: 6 SERVINGS

Erdener-Treppchen-Auslese is a good wine choice.

- 3 10-ounce whole trout, butterflied, cleaned, and boned, with heads and tails removed

Crabmeat Mayonnaise

1   egg
2   tablespoons fresh lemon juice
½   teaspoon salt
¼   teaspoon Dijon mustard
1   cup salad oil, olive oil, half of each
1   cup crabmeat, flaked and picked over carefully to re-
    move shell and cartilage

2   lemons, sliced, for garnish
¼   cup chopped fresh parsley, for garnish

Place the trout on grill under broiler, 4 inches from the heat. Broil 5–7 minutes. Gently turn trout midway through cooking time. *Do not overcook.* (Slightly undercooked fish is juicy and flavorful. Overcooking makes fish dry, tough, and tasteless.)

Prepare Crabmeat Mayonnaise: Place egg, lemon juice, salt, mustard, and 2 tablespoons of oil in blender. Blend on low speed for 5–6 seconds. Slowly pour in remaining oil in a steady stream, with blender at a very low speed. When oil is incorporated, cover and blend at high speed 4–5 seconds. Transfer the contents to a mixing bowl. With rubber spatula, fold in flaked crabmeat. Serve trout on platter garnished with sliced lemon and parsley. Pass the Crabmeat Mayonnaise at the table.

Fried Shrimp Louisiane

YIELD: 6 SERVINGS

Pour a Chateau St. Jean Chardonnay, Robert Young Vineyards, when serving this dish.

30	raw jumbo shrimp (approximately 2½ pounds)
1	medium onion, chopped
¼	lemon
1	teaspoon pickling spice
1	clove garlic, crushed
1	bay leaf
3	whole cloves
¼	teaspoon cayenne pepper
1	teaspoon salt

Batter

2	eggs
1	cup evaporated milk
½	teaspoon salt
2	cups fine bread crumbs
	Oil for frying

In a large soup pot, cover the shrimp with water. Add onion, lemon (before dropping in the ¼ lemon, give it a squeeze to allow the juice to mix with the water), pickling spice, garlic, bay leaf, cloves, cayenne, and 1 teaspoon salt. Bring to a boil, boil for 3-4 minutes until shrimp turn bright pink. Do not overcook. After shrimp are cooked, allow them to cool in the water in which they were boiled.

In a mixing bowl, prepare batter: Beat the eggs with the milk and ½ teaspoon salt until fluffy. Peel the cooled shrimp. Dip each shrimp into the egg batter, then into the bread crumbs, and repeat. Fry in deep, hot, pure oil that has reached a temperature of 390–400°F. Fry until golden brown, approximately 2–3 minutes. Serve with Tartar Sauce (page 20).

Variation: Boiled Shrimp Dinner

YIELD: 6 SERVINGS

Serve this with a mixed green salad and hot French bread with garlic butter. Provide plenty of shrimp. Also provide plenty of paper napkins, and it might be a good idea to ask that guests wear jeans. Try an Iron Horse Chardonnay with these simple, succulent shrimp.

Boil the shrimp as in Fried Shrimp Louisiane, but do not allow them to cool. It may be necessary to simmer the shrimp for a few minutes after boiling to complete the cooking. Do not peel; drain and serve at once, giving each guest a bowl for shrimp shells and a cup with melted butter for dipping.

Russian Cucumber Salad

YIELD: 6 SERVINGS

5	medium cucumbers, chopped fine
1	tablespoon vinegar
1	teaspoon salt
¼	teaspoon freshly ground black pepper
3	hard-cooked egg yolks
1	cup dairy sour cream

Combine the cucumbers with the vinegar, salt, and pepper. In another bowl, mash the egg yolks with the sour cream. Combine cucumbers with sour cream mixture. Refrigerate until ready to serve.

Poultry

The smooth texture and protein-rich, mild taste of chicken and its relatives are the pride and joy of the dinner table. Carefully and quickly prepared, whether gently poached or embellished with a savory sauce, the following recipes always bring warm compliments.

The fancies of diners at the Pink Adobe frequently take a poultry turn, and when the fancies become realities the meal is very likely to center around chicken breasts. With packaged breasts so readily available at your nearest supermarket, there is no end to the wonderful dishes you can create. Unless a recipe calls for poaching first, I find that the boneless and skinless breasts are the most convenient to use.

Arroz con Pollo

YIELD: 8–10 SERVINGS

This dish is pure Spanish in origin, but I've added to it my own southwestern accent. It should come out subtly flavored with the olive oil but completely free from oiliness. It is important that you use a very high-quality extra-virgin olive oil. A Spanish wine such as Marqués De Riscal Red Rioja goes well.

2	2½- to 3-pound frying chickens
3½	tablespoons extra-virgin olive oil
1	large onion, chopped
1	medium bell pepper, chopped
1	clove garlic, minced
2	whole green chiles, roasted and peeled (see page xiv), cut into strips
4	large tomatoes, chopped
¼	teaspoon saffron
5	whole cloves
	Salt and freshly ground black pepper to taste
2	quarts boiling water
1	pound raw long-grain rice
1	jigger (1½ ounces) dry sherry
1	cup fresh or frozen cooked green peas, for garnish
½	cup frozen or canned drained artichoke hearts, for garnish
1	4-ounce can pimientos, drained and sliced, for garnish

Preheat oven to 350°F. Disjoint and cut each chicken into 8 serving pieces (do not use backs or necks). Heat 2½ tablespoons of the olive oil in a 6-quart flame-proof heavy casserole dish or roaster. Brown chicken in casserole dish, turning often. Add to chicken the onion, bell pepper, garlic, chiles, and tomatoes. Season with the saffron, cloves, salt, and pepper. Cover with 2 quarts of boiling water and simmer until chicken is tender, about 1 hour. Add rice and cook until all the liquid is absorbed (about 25 minutes). Add sherry and the remaining olive oil. Cover and steam for 5 minutes. Garnish with peas, artichokes, and pimientos. Heat in oven until vegetables are hot, about 10 minutes.

Chicken Calvados

YIELD: 6 SERVINGS

No southwestern or Creole roots here—although Calvados is quite popular in Santa Fe—but I concocted this for a special luncheon party and it's often in demand.

6	6-ounce boneless, skinless chicken breast halves (approximately 2 pounds)
¼	cup flour
2	tablespoons butter
½	cup Calvados
	Salt and freshly ground black pepper to taste
¼	cup chopped celery
6	½-inch-thick slices peeled Delicious apple
1½	cups apple juice
1	tablespoon currant jelly
1	tablespoon cornstarch
1	tablespoon water
1	tablespoon fresh lemon juice

Preheat oven to 350°F. Dust chicken lightly with flour. Heat butter in 3-quart sauté pan and brown chicken in the butter. Add Calvados to chicken and ignite. When flames subside, remove chicken from pan and place in a 9-by-15-by-3-inch oblong casserole dish. Reserve pan juices. Sprinkle chicken lightly with salt and pepper. Sauté celery in remaining butter in pan and add to casserole dish. Place an apple slice on each chicken breast. Mix apple juice with currant jelly and pour over chicken. Cover tightly with foil and bake for 60 minutes. Remove chicken and place on serving dish. Mix together cornstarch, water, and lemon juice. Heat together the mixture remaining in the casserole dish and the cornstarch mixture, stirring constantly until thickened. Pour over chicken. Serve immediately.

Poached Chicken

Many of the poultry mainstays at the Pink Adobe call for poaching chicken breasts before using them in the recipes. This is the method to use when following recipes that specify poached chicken.

3	whole chicken breasts (about 2 pounds) *or* 1 3-pound broiler-fryer
3	cups water
1	teaspoon salt
1	small carrot, chopped coarse or whole
1	small onion, quartered
2	sprigs parsley
1	stalk celery, quartered

Put chicken into a 4-quart saucepan and cover with water. Bring to a boil and add all other ingredients. Cover pot and simmer for 45 minutes. Let chicken cool in broth. Remove chicken from pot, discard skin, and remove meat from bones in one piece. Strain broth. This stock is always nice to have in the refrigerator for soup and sauces. It also freezes well. Use one freezer container or freeze in ice cube trays and then store stock cubes in a plastic bag for use in small amounts.

Chicken Enchiladas with Sour Cream

YIELD: 6 SERVINGS (2 ENCHILADAS EACH)

Corona Extra beer goes perfectly with these creamy enchiladas.

2	whole chicken breasts, poached (page 82)
2	cups grated cheddar cheese
1	pint dairy sour cream

Green Chile Sauce

4	tablespoons olive oil
1	clove garlic, chopped
2	cups roasted, peeled, and chopped fresh green chiles (page xiv) or 1 16-ounce can chopped green chiles
5	medium ripe tomatoes, peeled and chopped (page xiv)
2	medium onions, chopped fine
½	teaspoon dried oregano
½	teaspoon salt
1	cup chicken broth (or enough to cover vegetables)

| ¼ | cup frying fat or lard |
| 12 | corn tortillas |

Preheat oven to 350°F. When chicken has thoroughly cooled from poaching, gently remove the meat and discard skin and bones. Shred meat into a bowl. Add half (1 cup) of the cheese and all the sour cream to the chicken and mix thoroughly. Set aside.

Prepare Green Chile Sauce: Heat olive oil in a 3-quart sauté pan. Add garlic and sauté until golden. Add chiles, tomatoes, onions, oregano, and salt. Add broth and cook over low heat until liquid is reduced by half (approximately 15 minutes). Set aside.

Melt fat in a 12-inch frying pan and fry tortillas one at a time until soft (only a few seconds per tortilla). Spread 6 tortillas on a flat surface. Divide chicken mixture in half and set one half aside. From other half, divide into six portions and spread on each tortilla. Put 2 tablespoons of the chile sauce mixture on each tortilla and roll. Repeat with the remaining 6 tortillas.

Place the rolls in a 9-by-13-by-2-inch baking pan, cover with the remaining sauce and cheese, and bake, uncovered, until thoroughly heated, about 15 minutes.

Garnish with chopped lettuce, Mexican style, and serve with Guacamole (p. 6).

Chicken Liza

YIELD: 6 SERVINGS

This simple but wonderful dish was named for my dear friend.
Uncork a Martin Vouvray and enjoy!

- 1½ sticks (12 tablespoons) butter
- 4 whole chicken breasts, poached (page 82)
- 6 small white onions, sliced paper-thin
  Salt and freshly ground black pepper to taste
- 1½ ounces fine cognac
- ½ teaspoon curry powder
- 3 cups heavy cream

Melt 1 stick (8 tablespoons) of the butter in a heavy 12-inch
skillet. Add chicken and onions, cover, and cook over low heat
for 20 minutes. Salt and pepper to taste, then add cognac, curry
powder, and cream. Simmer for 5 minutes. Place the chicken on
a plate, cover with foil, and keep warm in a very low-temperature
oven while you prepare the sauce: Place the sauce from the pan
into a blender and liquefy on high speed. Return to the skillet
and heat to *just below* the boiling point. Add remaining butter,
stir until melted, and pour over chicken. Serve.

Avocado and Chicken Casserole

YIELD: 6 SERVINGS

Robert Pecota Sauvignon Blanc '86 is a good wine choice.

1	cup broad flat green noodles
1	large ripe avocado, peeled and sliced
2	tablespoons fresh lime juice
½	cup butter
¼	cup flour
1	teaspoon salt
5	dashes Tabasco sauce
2¼	cups half-and-half
1	cup grated cheddar cheese
6	6-ounce boneless, skinless chicken breast halves, (approximately 2 pounds) poached (page 82)
½	cup roasted, peeled, and coarsely chopped fresh chiles (page xiv) or 1 4-ounce can whole green chiles, chopped coarse

Prepare noodles according to package directions, drain, and set aside. Preheat oven to 350°F. Drizzle avocado slices with lime juice and set aside. Melt butter in a 2-quart saucepan over low heat. Stir in flour, salt, and Tabasco over low heat until mixture bubbles. Add half-and-half slowly, stirring constantly until mixture thickens. Add cheese and stir until it has melted. Reserve 1 cup of this sauce. Mix remainder with cooked noodles. Place chicken in bottom of a 9-by-12-by-3-inch rectangular baking dish. Cover with chopped green chiles. Spoon noodle mixture over chicken and chiles. Place avocado slices on top and pour reserved sauce over avocados. Bake, uncovered, 35 minutes.

Sauté of Chicken Breasts Cilantro

YIELD: 8–10 SERVINGS

For the wine, try Sequoia Grove Chardonnay '84.

12 boneless, skinless chicken breast halves
   Salt and freshly ground black pepper to taste
¼ cup flour
4 tablespoons butter
¼ cup chicken stock

Cilantro Sauce

NOTE: Blanched almonds and/or walnuts may be substituted for piñons in the Cilantro Sauce. Also, a delicious variation is 1 cup piñons and 1 cup almonds.

2¼ cups firmly packed fresh cilantro
2 cups piñons (pine nuts) (see Note)
1½ cups grated Parmesan cheese
2 cloves garlic, peeled
¼ cup soft butter
1 cup plus 2 tablespoons olive oil

1½ pounds fettuccine noodles
4–6 tablespoons butter, for noodles
   Parmesan cheese, grated, for passing at table

Season chicken with salt and pepper. Roll in flour and shake off excess. In a heavy 12-inch skillet, heat butter. Add breasts and brown lightly on all sides. Add stock and cover skillet. Simmer for 10 minutes.

While chicken is simmering, prepare Cilantro Sauce: In a food processor fitted with steel blade, process 2 cups of cilantro, the piñons, Parmesan cheese, and garlic into a paste. Add softened butter. Slowly pour olive oil through feed tube until mixture is the consistency of heavy cream. Set aside.

Cook fettuccine according to package directions. Drain and place on a large platter. Toss with 4–6 tablespoons of butter. Toss in Cilantro Sauce, reserving some to use as a spread for the chicken. Place the chicken on a second platter and sprinkle with the remaining fresh cilantro. Serve with the remaining Cilantro Sauce on the side. Pass grated Parmesan at table.

Magic Package Chicken

YIELD: 6 SERVINGS

Alexander Valley Vineyards Chardonnay makes this entree even more magical.

4	tablespoons butter
2	tablespoons flour
½	cup milk
½	cup white wine or dry vermouth
½	cup chicken broth
1	egg yolk, beaten
1	dash cayenne pepper
1	dash ground nutmeg
1	dash ground cloves
4	tablespoons chopped fresh mushrooms
1	teaspoon chopped chives
6	chicken breast halves, poached (page 82)

Preheat oven to 375°F. Cut 6 pieces of aluminum foil large enough to make an envelope for each chicken breast. Butter the foil with half (2 tablespoons) of the butter. Make a paste with the remaining butter and the flour and set aside. Mix the milk, wine, and chicken broth together in a 1-quart saucepan and bring to a boil. Add the paste and stir until smooth. Reduce the heat to low; when boiling has stopped, gently stir in the egg yolk, being careful not to let the mixture boil. Remove from heat and add cayenne, nutmeg, cloves, mushrooms, and chives. Lay each chicken breast on a square of buttered foil; divide the sauce evenly over the breasts. Fold edges and seal together, but do not wrap too tightly around chicken. Bake for 10 minutes. Serve wrapped in the foil; guests open their own.

Dixieland Chicken Roll

YIELD: 6 SERVINGS

For that familiar, old-fashioned taste of creamed chicken and biscuits, this is the dish to serve. It is especially acceptable for an informal Sunday brunch. Serve with dishes of Pink Adobe Apricot Chutney (page 14). Green Chile Relish (page 19) and Tomato Sauce (page 21).

Filling

2	tablespoons butter
2	tablespoons flour
1	cup chicken stock (page 82)
½	teaspoon salt
⅛	teaspoon freshly ground black pepper
2	cups chopped cooked chicken
1	cup cooked green peas
1	tablespoon chopped pimiento

Dough

3	cups flour
4	teaspoons baking powder
1	teaspoon salt
2	tablespoons minced fresh parsley
½	cup plus 2–3 tablespoons lard
1¼	cups milk

Preheat oven to 350°F. Prepare the chicken filling: Mix the butter and flour to a paste consistency. In 2-quart saucepan, bring stock to slow boil. Add butter-flour paste and stir with a wire whisk until thickened. Add remaining filling ingredients, mix well, and set aside to cool.

Make Tomato Sauce and while sauce is cooking, prepare the dough:

Sift the flour, baking powder, and salt together into a mixing bowl. Add parsley and work in ½ cup lard. Add the milk slowly, stirring with a fork until the flour disappears. (You may not have to use all the milk.) Knead on a lightly floured board a few times and roll out until dough is about ⅓ inch thick. Spread the chicken filling on the dough and roll up like a jelly roll, pinching the ends of the dough together to seal. Brush the top of the roll with remaining 2–3 tablespoons melted lard and bake for 30–35 minutes. Place on a serving platter and cut into thick slices.

Poulet Marengo Pink Adobe

YIELD: 6 SERVINGS

Most gourmets are familiar with the legend of Poulet Marengo, the chicken dish that Napoleon's chef, Dunand (who he always took with him on campaigns), cooked on the battlefield after Napoleon defeated the Austrians in 1800. For the ingredients, the soldiers searched the ravaged land, finding only a small hen, a few tomatoes, a little garlic, and some crayfish. Dunand ingeniously put these meager rations together with a little brandy and gave it the name of the battle. While keeping the name and the basics from the original, I have embellished the dish with present-day extravaganza, and it's been received well at the Pink Adobe for years. Les Champs Gain Puligny Montrachet meets the high standards of this recipe.

1	cup plus 2 tablespoons flour
1	teaspoon salt
1	teaspoon paprika
3	2½- to 3-pound fryers, split in half
2	tablespoons butter
2	tablespoons olive oil
1	cup Madeira
1	clove garlic, chopped fine
	Bouquet garni
4–5	large fresh mushrooms, sliced
12	pitted black olives
1	8-ounce can whole onions
1	16-ounce can tomatoes
1	4-ounce can tomato juice
1	bay leaf
1	cup chicken broth

Garnish

1	4-ounce can pâté de foie gras with truffles
6	cooked shrimp, peeled and chopped
18	small croutons

Preheat oven to 325°F. Put 1 cup of flour, the salt, and paprika in large paper bag. Shake chicken halves, a few at a time, in this mixture until they are coated. In a heavy roaster, heat butter and oil and start browning the chicken halves (again, one or two at a time). Add a little more oil if necessary, but this dish should not be greasy. When halves are nicely browned (it is not necessary that chicken be cooked through), start packing the roaster.

Place 3 chicken halves in first layer, pressing them close together. Pour half the wine over the chickens. Distribute half the chopped garlic on each as well as a pinch of bouquet garni on each. Scatter half the mushrooms over the chickens. Place 2 olives on each and half the can of onions. Squeeze half the can of tomatoes over the first layer.

Place the three remaining chicken halves on this layer and repeat with remaining wine, seasonings, mushrooms, olives, onions, and tomatoes. Pour can of tomato juice over all and place bay leaf on top. Cover roaster tightly with foil. Bake for 2 hours. At the end of that time, remove foil and very carefully remove chickens to serving platter. They will be fork-tender, so be careful. Keep in warm place while making sauce.

With a wire whisk, mix remaining 2 tablespoons flour with the cup of chicken broth. Bring the juice in the roaster to a boil and beat in broth until it thickens. If too thick, thin the sauce with a little Madeira.

Just before serving, spread the pâté de foie gras on each chicken, as well as the chopped shrimp and croutons. Serve sauce separately.

Variation: Cotelletes de Porc Napoleon

YIELD: 6 SERVINGS

The perfect accompaniment with the dish is buttered green noodles. Chassagne Montrachet is a good wine choice.

Using 12 center-cut loin pork chops, 1 inch thick, pack the roaster or casserole as above. (It is best not to brown the chops quite as much as the chicken in the beginning step.) Cover tightly with foil and bake 2 hours. Omit the pâté de foie gras, shrimp, and croutons.

Sesame Chicken in Acorn Squash

YIELD: 4 SERVINGS

Try serving this with Bibb Lettuce with Grilled Brie Toast (page 41) and a bottle of Grgich Chardonnay.

Marinade

1	1-inch piece fresh gingerroot, peeled and sliced thin
2	tablespoons sesame oil
3	cloves garlic, peeled and halved
1	teaspoon chili powder
½	cup white wine
¼	cup soy sauce

Chicken

2	whole chicken breasts, cut into ¾-inch strips
2	acorn squash, halved lengthwise
½	cup flour
4	tablespoons sesame seeds
3	tablespoons unsalted butter
3	carrots, peeled, sliced, and blanched
20	snow peas, blanched
1	small head broccoli, cut and blanched

Combine marinade ingredients in a large bowl. Marinate chicken strips overnight.

Preheat oven to 350°F. Place squash cut side down in a 9-by-13-by-2-inch baking pan. Add approximately ½ inch water and bake squash until tender, about 40 minutes.

About 15 minutes before squash is done, combine flour and sesame seeds. Remove chicken from marinade and roll strips in this mixture.

Melt butter in skillet. Sauté chicken 4–5 minutes, until golden. Remove chicken. Pour off butter and crumbs. Add ¼ cup strained marinade to skillet. Stir in vegetables and cook until heated. Add chicken and combine thoroughly. Spoon chicken mixture into the baked squash halves.

Chicken Mezra with Red Chile Glaze

YIELD: 6 SERVINGS

Originally settled in 1600, the Barrio de Analco is the oldest settlement of European origin in Santa Fe. Some of the buildings still standing in this area probably were constructed during that time period. The Pink Adobe is one such building. It stands on the site of numerous Indian uprisings, and it is said that one room is inhabited by the friendly ghost of a young Indian servant maiden called Mezra. Legend has it that she has been seen and heard on many occasions. We honor her with this recipe.

½   cup flour
½   teaspoon salt
½   teaspoon freshly ground black pepper
6   6-ounce boneless, skinless chicken breast halves (approximately 2 pounds)
3   tablespoons butter
3   tablespoons olive oil
¼   cup very finely chopped celery
¼   cup very finely chopped onions
2   tablespoons chopped fresh parsley
¼   cup chicken stock
1   10-ounce jar red chile jelly
1   cup crumbled goat cheese (Montrachet)

In large bowl, combine flour, salt, and pepper. Roll chicken in flour mixture and shake off excess. In a heavy 12-inch skillet, heat butter and oil. Lightly sauté celery, onions, and parsley. Remove from pan with a slotted spoon and reserve. In same butter and oil, sauté chicken breasts until lightly browned (3–4 minutes per side). Sprinkle reserved sautéed vegetables on top of each chicken breast. Add chicken stock. Cover skillet and simmer for 5 minutes. Remove from heat and spread each chicken breast with red chile jelly. Place under broiler until jelly melts, basting often with melting jelly. Place chicken breasts on a large platter and sprinkle with goat cheese.

Chicken Tamale Pie

Yield: 6 servings

Dos Equis beer is the perfect beverage for this dish.

1	3- 4-pound frying chicken
1	carrot, peeled and chopped
4	sprigs stemless parsley, chopped
3	teaspoons salt
2⅛	cups yellow cornmeal
2	cups cold water
1	medium onion, chopped
1	clove garlic, minced
2	tablespoons minced bell pepper
¼	cup raisins
3½	tablespoons olive oil
1	cup chopped black olives
1	tablespoon hot chili powder
⅛	teaspoon saffron
	Salt and freshly ground black pepper to taste
1	28-ounce can tomatoes
2	cups cooked fresh corn (from approximately 4 ears) or 1 17-ounce can whole-kernel corn
1	cup sliced black olives, for garnish

Cover the chicken with cold water in a 4-quart pot. Add carrot, parsley, and 1 teaspoon of the salt. Bring to a boil, reduce heat, and simmer until tender (approximately 1 hour). Remove the chicken and strain the broth. When chicken is cool, pick meat from bones. Discard skin and bones. Shred the chicken meat.

Measure 6 cups of broth and bring to a boil. Mix 2 cups of the cornmeal with 2 cups of cold water. Stir the cornmeal mixture into the boiling broth, stirring constantly until it thickens. Season with remaining 2 teaspoons of salt and remove from heat. Keep in warm place, covered with foil.

Preheat oven to 350°F. In a 3-quart sauté pan, sauté onion, garlic, bell pepper, and raisins in 3 tablespoons of the olive oil until onion is wilted. Add the shredded chicken, chopped olives, chili powder, saffron, and salt and pepper to taste. Add tomatoes and corn. Mix well and add remaining ⅛ cup of cornmeal, stirring until mixture is slightly thick. Line a 3-quart casserole dish with the cornmeal mixture, pressing it with a spoon on the bottom of dish and up the sides. Reserve enough to cover the top. Fill with chicken mixture and trickle in the remaining ½ tablespoon of olive oil. Top with remaining cornmeal mush. Garnish with the sliced olives. Bake for 20–30 minutes.

Lasagna Monte

YIELD: 6 SERVINGS

1	pound lasagna noodles
2	pounds boneless, skinless chicken breasts, poached (page 82)
3	cups fresh green chiles, roasted, peeled, and cut in strips, (page xiv) or 1 27-ounce can whole green chiles
1½	cups ricotta cheese
1½	cups dairy sour cream
1	8-ounce package sliced mozzarella cheese
½	cup sliced pitted black olives

Preheat oven to 325°F. Cook noodles according to package directions. Place the first of three layers of noodles in a 9-by-15-inch buttered baking pan. Slice the poached chicken breasts and cover the noodles with half of the chicken. Cover chicken with half of the green chiles. Mix together ricotta cheese and sour cream. Spoon half of this mixture over green chiles. Repeat layering process beginning with the noodles. Then place the last layer of noodles on top. Cover with mozzarella slices and sprinkle with olives. Bake, uncovered, for 30 minutes.

Turkey Mole Poblano

YIELD: 6 SERVINGS

The secret of the food chemistry enigma in mole (moh-lay) is the use of chocolate, as well as a variety of chiles, spices, and nuts. Though it probably won't be as good, you can use prepared mole paste, available in specialty food shops, if you don't have time to make it yourself. Mole is a wonderful dish for special celebrations, and its highly distinctive flavor can certainly become habit-forming. It is equally delicious served with turkey or pork.

1	10-pound turkey, disjointed and cut into serving pieces
1	cup milk
1	cup flour
2	tablespoons cooking oil
½	pound pork (from loin or shoulder), diced into ½-inch pieces

Mole Sauce

8	cups boiling water
¼	pound large, dark, dried red chiles (ancho or mulato)
¼	pound long, thin, dried red chiles (pasillo)
½	pound light, dried red chiles (New Mexico)
½	cup blanched almonds
1	cup shelled piñons (pine nuts)
3	tablespoons lard
½	cup sesame oil
¼	teaspoon ground cloves
1	tablespoon ground cinnamon
2	ounces unsweetened chocolate, shaved
1	tablespoon sugar

Dip turkey pieces first in milk, then in flour. Shake off excess flour. Heat oil in a 4- to 6-quart Dutch oven or heavy skillet. Fry pork and turkey pieces together until well browned, turning turkey and stirring pork often.

While meat is browning, prepare Mole Sauce: Pour 2½ cups boiling water over chiles and soak for 20 minutes. Drain, slice open chiles, and discard seeds. Place chiles and nuts in a blender. Blend on high speed until mixture has a pastelike consistency. Heat 3 tablespoons of lard in a heavy 3-quart saucepan over moderate heat. Fry chile mixture in hot lard for 5 minutes, stirring constantly. Stir in sesame oil, spices, chocolate, and sugar. Fry for a few minutes, then add 2½ cups boiling water. Continue stirring until well blended. Remove from heat.

Place turkey and pork in a large 6-quart pot. Cover with chile mixture and the rest of the boiling water (3 cups). Cook for 1 hour at a simmer, *do not boil*. Stir occasionally. The sauce should be thick and creamy. Serve with hot Flour Tortillas (page 140).

Fried Turkey Lucifer
with Barbecue Sauce

YIELD: 6 SERVINGS

For a picnic on the patio, this unusual turkey platter is always received with great delight. An excellent accompaniment is Potato Salad with Green Chiles (page 50).

1	8-pound turkey
1	cup flour
4	teaspoons dry mustard
3	teaspoons salt
¼	teaspoon freshly ground black pepper
1	tablespoon chili powder
2	cups milk
	Cooking oil for frying
1	tablespoon Worcestershire sauce
1	clove garlic, crushed
1	dash Tabasco sauce
	Pink Adobe Barbecue Sauce (page 15)

Preheat oven to 350°F. Disjoint turkey and cut into 8 pieces: 2 legs, 2 thighs, 2 wings, 2 half breasts. Wings may be cut apart at the joint, which will give you 2 more pieces; the half breasts may be split in half for an additional 2 pieces. Mix together the flour, mustard, salt, pepper, and chili powder. Place in a large pie pan. Put milk in a deep bowl. Dip the turkey pieces first in milk and then in the dry mixture until well coated. Fill a 4- to 6-quart iron Dutch oven or large skillet 1½ inches deep with oil. Add Worcestershire sauce, crushed garlic, and Tabasco. Heat this mixture to 375°F. Add turkey pieces, a few at a time, being careful not to overcrowd. Cook until golden brown, about 25–30 minutes, flipping pieces midway through. Drain on paper towels. Place pieces in an oblong 10-by-15-by-4-inch baking pan. Brush each piece lightly with Pink Adobe Barbecue Sauce. Cover pan with foil and bake for 25–30 minutes.

Meat

Since there is a seemingly endless variety of cuts and kinds of meats, and even more ways of preparing them, I will give you only a few of my favorites.

Beef

Barbecue Beef Sandwich

YIELD: 6 SERVINGS

1	5- to 6-pound sirloin tip roast
	Salt and freshly ground black pepper to taste
3	tablespoons olive oil or bacon fat
2	large onions, chopped fine
2	ribs celery, chopped fine
2	cloves garlic, minced
1	28-ounce bottle catsup
1	16-ounce can stewed tomatoes
¼	cup vinegar
½	cup brown sugar
2	tablespoons chili powder
1	teaspoon chile pequin
1	pinch dried basil
1	pinch dried oregano
1	pinch ground cinnamon
1	teaspoon salt
½	teaspoon Tabasco sauce
¼	cup Worcestershire sauce
1	capful Liquid Smoke
	Bread

Preheat oven to 350°F. Salt and pepper roast. Brown well on all sides in oil in a Dutch oven. Remove meat from pot. Put onions, celery, and garlic into pot. Sauté until limp. Add remaining ingredients except bread. Simmer 5 minutes and return meat to pot. Spoon sauce over meat and bake for 3 hours. Remove from oven and cool. Refrigerate for one or two days. Remove meat and slice or shred very thin. Return to sauce. Heat over low heat for 1 hour. Serve on favorite bread.

Beef Stew Elaborate

YIELD: 6 SERVINGS

This may be called stew, but it is elaborate enough for the most delicate palate. Top round may be substituted for the tenderloin tip, but only at the sacrifice of quality. For the wine, pour a Chalone Pinot Noir.

½   teaspoon salt
½   teaspoon freshly ground black pepper
½   cup flour
2   pounds tenderloin tip, cut into 1½-inch cubes
2   tablespoons olive oil
1   cup beef stock
1   bay leaf
1   clove garlic, chopped
1   pinch dried rosemary
½   cup butter
1   3-inch fresh green chile pepper, chopped coarse
6   small whole onions
2   fresh tomatoes, quartered
2   medium potatoes, chopped very coarse
1   tablespoon chopped fresh parsley
2   cups red wine

Combine the salt, pepper, and flour in a large plastic bag. Add meat cubes to bag and coat well. Heat the olive oil in a deep iron skillet or a Dutch oven. Add meat to oil and brown slowly. Add the beef stock, bay leaf, garlic, and rosemary. Cover tightly. Simmer for 10 minutes, turning the meat often. In a separate skillet, melt the butter. Combine all the vegetables and brown in the butter. Pour the browned vegetables over the meat and add the wine to the meat skillet. Simmer until the meat is very tender, about 2 hours.

The Best Brisket of Beef

YIELD: 6 SERVINGS

Silverado Cabernet Sauvignon does justice to the brisket.

1   5-pound center-cut fresh brisket of beef

Marinade

1   large clove garlic, minced
½   teaspoon salt
½   teaspoon dried thyme
¼   teaspoon freshly ground black pepper
¼   cup olive oil

Roasting Vegetables

2   cups chopped (cored but not peeled) fresh tomatoes
1   8-ounce can Italian plum tomatoes, drained
1   cup chopped fresh green chiles
1½   cups sliced onion

Sauce

¼   cup red wine
1½   tablespoons cornstarch
¼   teaspoon salt
¼   teaspoon freshly ground black pepper

Trim fat off brisket. Make a paste of garlic, salt, thyme, and pepper in food processor. Pour in oil and process a bit longer. Spread this over both sides of brisket. Marinate overnight.

Preheat oven to 300°F. Place roast in a wide 4-quart heavy roasting pan. Cover meat with roasting vegetables. Cover tightly and roast for 3–4 hours, basting meat with accumulated juices every half hour. The meat is done when a fork pierces it quite easily. Transfer roast and vegetables to a smaller pan. Degrease roasting juices (skim grease off top using a baster) and pour into a 1-quart saucepan. Simmer juices.

Mix together sauce ingredients and whisk into simmering juices. Simmer 2–3 minutes. Pour over brisket.

Dobeburger

YIELD: 6 SERVINGS

An experiment with herbs, spices, and condiments resulted in a delightful sauce that we named Dobe Sauce; so, when this is poured over a chopped beef patty, a Dobeburger results. Dobeburgers were one of the first Pink Adobe menu offerings and a favorite for more than 40 years.

1½	pounds fresh ground round steak
1	cup mayonnaise (page 54)
¼	cup Worcestershire sauce
½	teaspoon Tabasco sauce
1	generous dash dried savory
½	cup catsup
1	sprinkle each garlic salt and celery salt
6	hamburger buns

Form ground round into 6 patties and broil to desired doneness. In a small bowl, mix all other ingredients together to make a smooth sauce. Serve over cooked patties on toasted buttered buns.

Santa Fe Meat Loaf

YIELD: 6 SERVINGS

Caymus Zinfandel '84 makes this meat loaf even better.

1   pound meat loaf mix (¼ pound ground veal, ¼ pound ground pork, ½ pound ground beef)
1   11-ounce can Mandarin orange segments, drained
1   egg
1   slice homemade-style bread, soaked in ¼ cup half-and-half
2   cups piñons (pine nuts)
½   teaspoon salt
1   teaspoon chili powder
1   teaspoon chopped jalapeño pepper
¼   teaspoon garlic salt
¼   cup green chile jelly

Sauce

2   tablespoons butter
½   cup chopped onion
¼   cup chopped celery
1   tablespoon flour
1   10½-ounce can condensed beef bouillon
¼   cup sherry
2   tablespoons green chile jelly

Preheat oven to 350°F. Combine all meat loaf ingredients, excluding jelly. Blend well and press into a 9-by-5-by-4-inch loaf pan. Melt ¼ cup jelly (easiest to microwave for 1 minute in a glass cup) and pour over loaf to glaze. Bake for 1 hour.

Prepare sauce: Heat butter in heavy skillet and sauté onion and celery until limp. Stir in flour and slowly add bouillon, sherry, and 2 tablespoons jelly. Simmer until mixture thickens, about 8 minutes. Serve on side of meat loaf.

Steak Dunigan

YIELD: 2 SERVINGS

This was named for its inventor, Pat Dunigan, who insisted on adding green chiles to his steak. There was soon such a demand for it I had to put it on the menu! Robert Mondavi Cabernet Sauvignon Reserve is very good with this zesty steak.

Green Chile Sauce

1	medium onion, chopped fine
2	tablespoons olive oil
2	4-ounce cans green chiles, drained and chopped
¼	teaspoon dried oregano
¼	teaspoon minced fresh cilantro
¼	teaspoon salt
1	teaspoon Tabasco sauce or chopped jalapeño pepper

Steak

4	large fresh mushrooms, sliced thin
4	tablespoons butter
	Hickory-smoked salt (Spice Island or Schilling is best) to taste
2	14- to 15-ounce top-grade New York cut sirloin steaks

Prepare Green Chile Sauce: First sauté onion in oil. Add remaining sauce ingredients and cook for 5 minutes. Keep warm in very low-temperature oven.

Sauté mushrooms in butter until soft, approximately 5 minutes. Remove from pan and also keep warm in oven. Shake hickory salt on both sides of steaks. Broil or grill to desired doneness, (10–15 minutes for rare; 15–20 minutes for medium), turning once.

Transfer steaks to platter. Divide mushrooms over top of steaks. Cover each with Green Chile Sauce.

Pork

Barbecued Baby Back Ribs

YIELD: 6 SERVINGS

This three-step method of cooking ribs results in the most tender of all rib barbecuing. When buying ribs, always plan on one pound per person. Silver Oak Cabernet Sauvignon '82 is a good wine choice.

6	pounds baby back ribs, cut into sections of 2–3 ribs each
1	medium onion, chopped
1	clove garlic, crushed
1	tablespoon hot red pepper flakes
1	teaspoon whole peppercorns
1	tablespoon salt
2	quarts Pink Adobe Barbecue Sauce (page 15)

Preheat oven to 325°F. Place ribs in a 4- to 6-quart stockpot. Cover ribs with water. Add onion, garlic, red pepper, peppercorns, and salt and bring to a boil. Lower heat and simmer for an hour. Drain. Place ribs in 2 separate 15-by-8-inch baking pans, one layer of ribs in each. Be sure ribs are packaged closely together. Into each pan pour 2 cups of Pink Adobe Barbecue Sauce, turning ribs to coat. Cover pans tightly with foil and bake for an hour. Remove foil and place one pan at a time under broiler, approximately 4 inches from heat. Broil until the edges turn crisp and are browned, about 5–10 minutes. While broiling, it's important to turn ribs to assure even browning. Serve ribs with the remaining barbecue sauce on the side.

Garden of Eden Pork Roast

YIELD: 6 SERVINGS

Mont Redon White Chateauneuf-du-Pape is an appropriate selection. Caramelized Onions or Caramelized New Potatoes (page 126) would be a good accompaniment.

½ teaspoon salt
½ teaspoon grated orange peel
½ teaspoon grated lemon peel
1 teaspoon coarsely ground black pepper
1 teaspoon dried thyme
1 3-pound boneless pork loin
½ cup fresh orange juice
½ cup apple juice
2 tablespoons Grand Marnier
1 14-ounce can chicken broth
1 golden Delicious apple, cored and sliced (1 cup)
1 medium onion, sliced (1 cup)
1 tablespoon chopped jalapeño pepper
1½ tablespoons cornstarch
¼ cup water

Preheat oven to 350°F. Combine salt, orange peel, lemon peel, pepper and thyme in small mixing bowl. Rub mixture into skin of roast, pressing with force. Place the roast on a rack in a 9-by-12-inch roasting pan. Cook for 1 hour or until roast has reached an internal temperature of 145°F. Pour off drippings. Add juices, Grand Marnier, broth, apple, onion, and jalapeño to the roast in the pan. Bake for an additional 30 minutes or until roast has reached an internal temperature of 160°F. Transfer meat to a serving platter. Combine cornstarch and water in a small bowl and mix well. In a 4-quart saucepan, bring juices from roasting pan to a boil. Stir in cornstarch mixture and bring to a slow boil. Pour juices over meat and serve.

Ham Baked in Bag

YIELD: 6 SERVINGS

I can remember my mother cooking turkeys and hams in bags long before cooking bags were introduced. There's nothing like fresh baked him in a bag, tender and succulent almost beyond belief. A Red Hermitage goes well with baked ham.

1 16-pound fully cooked bone-in ham
1 large (17-by-12-inch) heavy brown supermarket paper bag

Preheat oven to 350°F. Slide ham into paper bag. Fold edges over tightly or staple. Place bag in oblong pan large enough to hold bag, at least 18 by 13 by 6 inches. Bake for an hour. Remove from oven and very carefully slit bag. Allow the steam to escape. Be careful! Steam can burn. When cool enough to handle, tear off remaining bag. Pour off fat. Using a sharp knife, remove all skin and fat. Serve thinly sliced.

Variation: Ham Glazed with Apricot

YIELD: 6 SERVINGS

This can be a very festive dish when served on a large platter garnished with fruit and flowers. Nasturtiums are especially compatible. For the wine, try Red Hermitage.

1 16-pound fully cooked bone-in ham
Whole cloves

Apricot Glaze

1 11-ounce jar apricot preserves
1 tablespoon grated orange rind

Preheat oven to 350°F. Prepare ham according to directions for Ham Baked in Bag above. Increase oven temperature to 400°F. Instead of slicing ham at the end, score the top of ham in diamond patterns about ½ inch deep. Place a whole clove in the corner of each diamond.

Prepare Apricot Glaze: Place apricot preserves in a 1½-quart saucepan. Bring to a slow boil, stirring constantly. Cook about 5 minutes, until liquefied. Place in sieve over a large bowl and press pulp until all juice is extracted. Stir in orange rind. Brush glaze over ham and return to oven. Bake, uncovered, for 15 minutes, basting if necessary as glaze melts.

Curried Stuffed Pork Chops

YIELD: 6 SERVINGS

Try Mount Veeder Chenin Blanc.

6	double pork loin chops
	Salt and freshly ground black pepper to taste
1	lemon
1½	cups dry bread crumbs
½	cup piñon nuts
1	teaspoon minced onion
1	tablespoon finely chopped tart apple
	Dash cayenne pepper
	Pinch dried thyme
1	teaspoon curry powder or to taste
½	cup milk (approximately)

Preheat oven to 350°F. Be sure the chops are lean, fairly large, and cut so that each chop is split through and joined at the bone. Salt and pepper each chop inside and out and rub juice from the lemon on the outside. In large bowl, mix remaining ingredients together, using enough milk to make the stuffing moist but not soggy. Fill the pork chops with stuffing mix. Place chops in a 9-by-12-by-2-inch casserole dish. Cover. Bake for 1 hour. If not brown after this time, remove cover and increase heat. Serve with Pink Adobe Apricot Chutney (page 14).

Red Chile with Pork

YIELD: 6 SERVINGS

Quench your thirst with Dos Equis.

- ¼ cup olive oil
- 2 pounds boneless pork, cut into 1-inch pieces
- ¼ cup flour
- 1 tablespoon chili powder
- 1 teaspoon salt
- ½ cup coarsely chopped onion
- 1 clove garlic, minced
- ½ teaspoon dried oregano
- ¾ cup beef broth
- 1½ cups Fresh Red Chile Sauce (page 18)

Heat oil in a 12-inch Dutch oven. In a paper bag, shake pork with flour, chili powder, and salt. Brown pork lightly in oil, turning often. Add onion and garlic and stir. Mix in oregano. Add broth, cover pot, and simmer for 5–10 minutes. Add Fresh Red Chile Sauce and mix well. Cover pot again and simmer for 35–45 minutes, until pork is very tender.

Sunday Night (or Morning) Sausage Patties

YIELD: 6 SERVINGS

These are appropriate for Sunday evening or midnight snack. But together with the Creole Calas (page 136) and a pot of French coffee, they'll give you a real New Orleans breakfast.

3	slices bread
1	pound pork sausage
1	onion, chopped fine
1	egg
¼	teaspoon salt
¼	teaspoon freshly ground black pepper
	Dash ground cloves
	Dash ground cinnamon
½	cup water
1	cup seedless grapes cut into halves

Remove crusts from the bread; break bread into small pieces. Mix remaining ingredients together thoroughly with bread, adding grapes last. Form into patties and sauté as you would any other sausage.

Lamb

Lamb Chops with White Wine

YIELD: 6 SERVINGS

Chateau Ducru Beaucaillou goes with these lamb chops.

- 4 tablespoons butter
- 6 loin lamb chops
- 2 tablespoons minced shallots
- 2 tablespoons chopped fresh parsley
- 1 tablespoon flour
- 1 cup white wine

Preheat oven to 325°F. Place half (2 tablespoons) the butter in a large heavy skillet and brown the chops on both sides. Remove the chops and keep warm in a baking dish large enough to allow them to lie flat and close together. Lightly sauté the shallots and parsley in the skillet. Add the flour and slowly thin with the white wine, stirring constantly. Pour over the chops and dot with the remaining butter. Seal the pan with aluminum foil and bake for 20 minutes. Remove foil and bake for another 5 minutes.

A NOTE ABOUT LAMB: *In northern New Mexico, the most widely used meat is pork, although "cabrito" (young goat) is a favorite too—usually roasted whole on a spit over an open pit. Lamb, though, is also raised in New Mexico and is quite popular. In the milder states, lambs are born in the early fall and are ready for the market in the spring. In the high country most lambs are born in the winter or early spring and are not available for market until five or six months later. This means that, thanks to today's ease of shipping, we have tender and delicious lamb all year long.*

Lamb should almost never be roasted at a temperature over 325° (300° is even better), for at a higher temperature the hard fat of lamb exudes an unpleasant odor. The exception, however, is broiled lamb chops, for they should be broiled quickly under high heat to produce succulent and juicy pink chops.

Lamb Curry

Preston Dry Chenin Blanc is good with curry.

¼	pound butter
2	medium onions, chopped fine
4	tart apples, peeled, cored, and chopped
¼	cup seedless raisins
1	5- to 6-pound boned leg of lamb
¼	cup curry powder
1	tablespoon cayenne pepper
¼	cup fresh lemon juice
¼	teaspoon ground ginger
⅛	teaspoon dried thyme
1	tablespoon salt
4	fresh tomatoes, chopped coarse
2	cups cooked kidney beans
2	tablespoons flour
¼	cup milk
3	cups cooked rice
	Ground peanuts, for garnish
	Shredded coconut, for garnish
	Pink Adobe Apricot Chutney (page 14), for garnish

Melt butter in a large pot and gently sauté the onions, apples, and raisins for 5–6 minutes. Remove all skin, sinews, and fat from lamb. Dice meat into small chunks. Place in pot along with sautéed mixture and add curry powder, cayenne, lemon juice, ginger, thyme, salt, and tomatoes. Cover with water or stock and cook, over low heat, covered, for 2 hours, or until lamb is very tender. When done, add kidney beans.

In mixing bowl, blend flour with the milk and some of the juice from the pot (not to exceed ¼ cup). Stir to thicken and add to pot. Serve over hot fluffy rice. Cover with peanuts, coconut, and small pieces of chutney.

Fabulous Braised Leg of Lamb

YIELD: 6 SERVINGS

When time is not the primary consideration, this method of cooking lamb produces the most succulent, tender, delicious lamb I have ever tasted. The result is well worth the time, care, and attention required. The preliminary cooking may be done the day before. This leg of lamb pairs well with Chateau Pichon Lalande Grand Cru '83.

    1   tablespoon butter
    1   tablespoon olive oil
    2   large onions, sliced
    2   large carrots, sliced
    1   stalk celery, sliced
    3–4 sprigs parsley
    ¼   teaspoon dried thyme
    1   bay leaf
    1   6-pound leg of lamb, boned, rolled and tied (save bones)
    3   tomatoes, chopped
    1½   cups beef broth
    1   cup strong black coffee
    1   tablespoon cornstarch
    ¼   cup Madeira

Preheat oven to 325°F. Place butter and oil in a large heavy oval 13-by-10-by-5-inch roaster. Spread onions, carrots, celery, parsley, thyme, and bay leaf over oil. Place lamb bones over vegetables, then the rolled lamb over bones. Cook meat ½ hour in the oven, turning often, until it is browned evenly all over. Add tomatoes, broth, and coffee and cover with an oval piece of buttered waxed paper or parchment paper with a few fork holes punched in paper to allow the steam to vent. Cover with top of roaster.

Lower oven temperature to 300°F and cook for at least 4 hours, basting often with broth, adding more broth if necessary (a little at a time). Do *not* add more coffee, only broth. At end of cooking time, remove roast from pan. Discard bones. Strain gravy and transfer to saucepan. Taste for seasoning. In small bowl, mix cornstarch and wine. Add mixture to gravy to thicken. Stir to mix well. Serve lamb with gravy on side.

Peppery Lamb Stew

YIELD: 6 SERVINGS

Guigal Cotes-du-Rhone is a good wine choice.

2	tablespoons cooking oil
2	pounds lean lamb, cut into 1-inch cubes (preferably from leg of lamb)
2	teaspoons sugar
1	teaspoon salt
¼	teaspoon freshly ground black pepper
¼	cup flour
1	garlic clove, crushed
1	pound fresh tomatoes, peeled and chopped coarse (page xiv)
⅛	teaspoon dried rosemary
⅛	teaspoon dried thyme
1	bay leaf
1	cup chicken stock (approximately)
1½	cups dry vermouth
12	small new potatoes, peeled
2	cups peeled and sliced carrots (1-inch slices)
1	medium turnip, peeled and quartered
12	whole boiling onions, peeled
1	10-ounce package frozen peas
1	cup roasted, peeled, and coarsely chopped fresh green chiles (page xiv)
¼	cup minced fresh parsley, for garnish

Preheat oven to 325°F. Heat oil in a heavy 4-quart roaster. Brown meat on all sides. Drain off excess fat. Sprinkle meat with sugar, salt, and pepper. Mix and cook for 1 minute. Sprinkle with flour. Add garlic, tomatoes, rosemary, thyme, and bay leaf. Add chicken stock to cover just barely. Bring to a boil and cover. Transfer roaster to oven and bake 1½–2 hours, until tender. Add the vermouth a little at a time throughout the entire cooking period. Add potatoes, carrots, turnip, and onions. Cover and bake for 25 minutes longer. Add peas and green chiles and cook an additional 5 minutes. Garnish dish with fresh parsley.

Veal

Rolled Stuffed Breast of Veal New Mexican

YIELD: 8 TO 10 SERVINGS

A perfect dish for a stylish buffet! Although this dish is time consuming, the results are well worth the effort. Try Pinot Grigio, a dry white Italian wine, with veal.

4	pounds breast of veal (boned, reserve bones)
2	teaspoons salt
1	teaspoon freshly ground black pepper
¼	teaspoon ground coriander
1	pound chorizo sausage
¼	cup minced onions
¼	cup chopped piñon nuts
½	cup dry bread crumbs
1	cup roasted, peeled, and chopped fresh green chiles (page xiv)
1	egg, beaten
3	tablespoons cooking oil
1	cup thinly sliced onion
1	clove garlic, minced
1–2	cups jalapeño jelly
	Fresh mint and watercress for garnish
	String and cheesecloth

Pound the veal flat. Rub veal with salt, pepper, and coriander. Mix together sausage meat, onions, piñon nuts, bread crumbs, green chiles, and beaten egg. Spread over the veal and roll up veal like a jelly roll. Tie securely in several places with string.

Heat oil in a 4-quart Dutch oven and brown veal roll on all sides. Remove the veal roll, cool slightly, then wrap in cheesecloth and again tie securely. To the fat in the pan add the sliced onion and garlic. Cook five minutes. Return the veal (in cheesecloth) to the pot, add veal bones and enough water to reach halfway up the meat. Bring to a boil, cover, and cook over very low heat for 3 hours or until veal is tender. Let cool in liquid. Drain veal roll well and chill overnight.

Carefully remove cheesecloth and strings. Place the veal roll on a platter. Slice in ½-inch pieces. Garnish with fresh mint and watercress and place bowl of jalapeño jelly next to platter for guests to mask veal to their tastes.

Breaded Veal Cutlets with Fried Egg and Chile

YIELD: 6 SERVINGS

1½ pounds veal cutlet, cut in 6 uniform pieces and pounded very thin
¼   cup flour
½   cup dry bread crumbs
1½ teaspoons salt
1   cup milk
¼   pound butter
6   eggs
6   whole fresh green chiles, roasted and peeled
    Garnishes: lemon wedges, chopped parsley, fresh cilantro

NOTE: This dish is equally good prepared with pounded and flattened chicken breasts in place of veal.

Mix together flour, bread crumbs, and salt. Dip the veal pieces in milk, then in flour mixture, coating thoroughly. Melt half the butter in a 12-inch skillet over low heat. Cook veal in butter in a single layer until browned on both sides. Transfer to an oven-proof platter and keep warm in a 225°F oven while preparing remaining veal. Arrange veal in a single layer on serving platter. Fry eggs in remaining butter to desired doneness. Place a chile on each cutlet and top with a fried egg. Garnish with lemon wedge, chopped parsley, and a sprig of fresh cilantro.

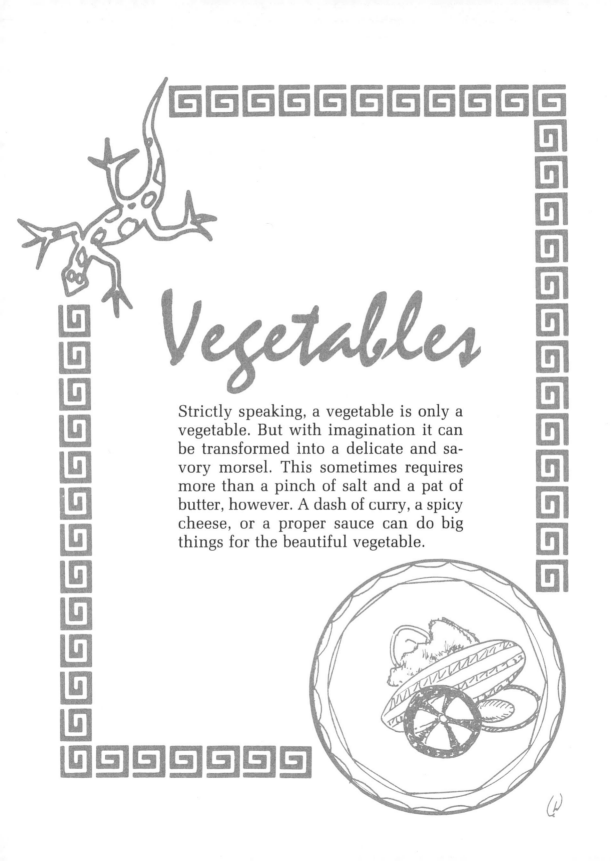

Vegetables

Strictly speaking, a vegetable is only a vegetable. But with imagination it can be transformed into a delicate and savory morsel. This sometimes requires more than a pinch of salt and a pat of butter, however. A dash of curry, a spicy cheese, or a proper sauce can do big things for the beautiful vegetable.

Asparagus Soufflé

1   pound fresh asparagus, or 1 9-ounce package frozen cut asparagus
6   tablespoons flour
4   tablespoons butter
3   eggs, separated
1½ cups milk
1   teaspoon salt
    Dash cayenne pepper
2   tablespoons minced pimientos
2   tablespoons minced bell pepper
2   tablespoons minced celery
1   tablespoon minced onion

Preheat oven to 350°F. Steam the asparagus until crisp-tender. While it is cooking, blend together the flour and butter. Separately beat the egg whites until stiff and the egg yolks until thick. Drain the asparagus, saving the liquid, and keep warm, covered, in low-temperature oven. Heat ½ cup of the reserved liquid with the milk over low to moderate heat and thicken with the flour paste. Stir constantly until smooth and creamy. Remove from heat. Stir in the egg yolks, salt, cayenne, vegetables, and cooked asparagus. Gently fold in the egg whites. Pour into a well-greased mold or 2-quart casserole dish and bake until browned and well risen, about 1 hour.

Buttered Parsley Asparagus

YIELD: 6 SERVINGS

In season, asparagus in New Mexico is plentiful and delicious. I often serve it steamed, chilled, and unadulterated. For a change, though, the following light sauce is a delightful complement.

2 pounds fresh asparagus
  Approximately 2½ cups of salted water
¼ pound butter
¾ cup parsley, chopped
1 cup Parmesan cheese, grated

Wash asparagus and break off tough ends. Stand on end in a tall, narrow pot or asparagus cooker with a tight fitting lid. Add salted water to half cover asparagus. Cover tightly and cook at a slow boil until crisp but tender—8–10 minutes. Do not overcook. While asparagus is cooking, prepare sauce: melt butter in a 1-quart saucepan and heat almost to the point of burning. Stir in parsley. Drain asparagus, place on a hot platter, and cover with the butter-parsley sauce. Sprinkle with Parmesan cheese and serve.

NOTE: This upright method of boiling assures uniformity. The tender tips steam while the stalks boil.

Santa Fe Corn Soufflé

YIELD: 6 SERVINGS

2 cups fresh corn on the cob (see Note)
5 tablespoons butter
¼ cup finely chopped onion
3 large eggs, separated
¼ cup roasted, peeled, and chopped fresh green chiles (page xiv)
½ teaspoon salt

Preheat oven to 375°F. Using 2 tablespoons of the butter, grease a 1½-quart soufflé dish. Sprinkle dish lightly with flour. This will prevent soufflé from sticking. Set aside. In a medium skillet, sauté onion in remaining butter until soft. In food processor, combine egg yolks, onion, and corn. Process until corn is fine. Transfer to a large bowl. Stir in chiles and salt. Beat egg whites until stiff. With a rubber spatula, fold gently but thoroughly into corn mixture. Scrape into prepared soufflé dish. Bake 10 minutes, then reduce heat to 350°F and bake 30 minutes longer, until lightly browned and when a knife inserted in center comes out clean.

NOTE: Two cups (16 ounces) of canned yellow kernel corn may be substituted for fresh corn, but I do not advise it.
To cut kernels from cobs, stand cob on end in a pie tin and slice downward, away from yourself, using a sharp knife. Scrape the milk from the cobs with the dull edge of the knife.

Stuffed Beets

YIELD: 6 SERVINGS

1   10-ounce can medium whole beets, with juice
½   cup vinegar
½   cup water
    Salt and sugar to taste
6   hard-cooked eggs, chopped fine
3   teaspoons chopped chives
3   teaspoons chopped fresh parsley
1   cup mayonnaise (page 54)
1   teaspoon dry mustard
½   teaspoon grated onion
    Salt and freshly ground black pepper to taste

Drain the beets, reserving the juice. Hollow out the beets, using a melon cutter or sharp spoon, until the shells are fairly thin. Cover the shells with the vinegar, water, and ½ cup of the beet juice. Let stand—a day or two is not too long. Add salt and sugar to taste. Mix eggs, chives, and parsley together. Blend in mayonnaise, mustard, and onion. Add salt and pepper to taste. Fill the beets just before serving time. Serve cool.

Variation

Marinate the beet shells in the juice from a jar of sweet pickles.

Chile Rellenos

YIELD: 6 SERVINGS

12 large green chiles, with stems, roasted and peeled (page xiv)
1 pound Monterey Jack cheese, cut into 12 even strips
¼ cup chopped yellow onion
Oil for deep frying

Batter

½ cup flour
½ teaspoon baking soda
½ teaspoon salt
2 tablespoons flat beer
2 eggs, separated
1–2 tablespoons water

Cut a small slit below the stem of each pepper and remove seeds. Stuff each chile carefully, to avoid breaking it, with 1 piece of cheese and 1 teaspoon onion. Heat deep frying oil to 375°F.

To prepare batter, blend together dry ingredients. Beat together beer and egg yolks. Combine with dry ingredients. Add only enough water to make a very light batter (consistency of pancake batter). Beat egg whites until stiff and frothy. Fold whites into batter. Dip stuffed chiles, one by one, into batter. Deep-fry until golden brown.

Variations

Instead of the Monterey Jack and onions, try these stuffing variations:
1. piñon (pine nuts), golden raisins, and cheddar cheese
2. banana strips with pureed walnut meat
3. ½ pound well-seasoned ground meat, cooked, and cheddar or goat cheese
4. chicken breast strips, cooked, and chopped onions

Corn Pudding

YIELD: 6 SERVINGS

1 cup cooked corn kernels
3 eggs, well beaten
¼ teaspoon salt
¼ teaspoon brown sugar
  Dash freshly ground black pepper
¾ cup milk
½ cup heavy cream
1 tablespoon melted butter

Preheat oven to 325°F. In a large bowl, mix all ingredients and place in a buttered 1½-quart casserole dish. Bake for 45 minutes to an hour (or until pudding sets). Serve warm.

Carnival Okra

YIELD: 6 SERVINGS

1 pound fresh okra
2 ears fresh corn on the cob
3 tablespoons bacon fat
1 medium onion, chopped
1 large fresh tomato, chopped
  Salt and freshly ground black pepper to taste
1 cup beef broth

Cut the stems from the okra and discard. Cut pods crosswise into ¾-inch rounds. Cut and scrape kernels off corn cobs. Heat fat in 3-quart sauté pan. Add okra, corn, onion, and tomato. Fry for about 5 minutes, stirring often. Add salt and pepper. Reduce heat and add just enough broth to keep vegetables from sticking. Cover and cook for 20–25 minutes, stirring in more broth as needed. Serve warm.

Cream and Butter Corn

YIELD: 6 SERVINGS

3   cups fresh corn (6–8 ears)
¼   pound butter
1   tablespoon minced bell pepper
     Salt and freshly ground black pepper to taste
16   ounces half-and-half

Melt butter in a 12-inch skillet. Add corn, bell pepper, salt, and pepper. Stir and cook for 5 minutes. Do not overcook. Add half-and-half and reduce heat to simmer. When cream has cooked away, about 7–10 minutes, serve hot.

Balsamic Spinach and Bacon Skillet

YIELD: 6 SERVINGS

1½–2 pounds fresh spinach
5   slices bacon
2   tablespoons balsamic vinegar
½   teaspoon salt
¼   teaspoon freshly ground black pepper

Remove stems and ribs from spinach and wash leaves with cold water; do not dry leaves. Place in 2-quart pot with tight-fitting lid. Cook in water that clings to leaves for 3–5 minutes. Drain well. Fry bacon in a 10-inch skillet until crisp. Remove bacon and drain on a paper towel. Remove all but 2 tablespoons of drippings from skillet. Add spinach to drippings along with vinegar, salt, and pepper. Stir well. Crumble bacon over all. Serve immediately.

Caramelized Onions

For a tantalizing taste experience, try caramelizing vegetables. This simple method gives a delicious, interesting flavor, especially to boiled onions and boiled new potatoes. Both of these dishes are very compatible with a succulent Garden of Eden Pork Roast (page 107).

12   small onions, (about 1½ inches in diameter)

Caramel Sauce

1   cup beef broth
1½ cups brown sugar
1   tablespoon Madeira

Cut a cross in the root ends of the onions. Place in a 3-quart saucepan with enough boiling salted water to cover onions. When the onions are tender but still firm (25–30 minutes), remove from water and drain. The skins should slip off quickly and easily. Set aside.

Prepare Caramel Sauce: In a 2-quart saucepan, combine the broth, sugar, and wine. Stir constantly over low heat until sugar has dissolved and mixture coats spoon. Gently stir in onions and cook a few minutes, until onions are well coated and have a shiny brown color.

Variation: Caramelized New Potatoes

YIELD: 6 SERVINGS

Using 12 medium new potatoes, as uniform in size as possible, instead of onions, cook potatoes in a 4-quart saucepan in boiling salted water until tender (about 25 minutes). Remove skins. Prepare Caramel Sauce as for the Caramelized Onions and follow same procedure, coating only a few potatoes at a time until all are coated. Keep the potatoes warm by placing on a platter in a very low-temperature oven.

French-Fried Onions

YIELD: 6 SERVINGS

Real Bermuda onions are hard to obtain in most parts of the country, but good large onions of any kind are delicious when served this way.

6   large Bermuda onions
1   cup milk
1   cup flour
1   teaspoon salt
½   teaspoon freshly ground black pepper
     Fat for deep frying

Peel the onions and slice about ⅛-inch thick. Gently separate into whole rings and place in deep bowl. Cover with milk and refrigerate for an hour. Mix the flour, salt, and pepper thoroughly. Dip the onion rings alternately in this and the milk and repeat. Heat fat to 375°F and fry the rings until golden brown. Drain on paper towels and serve quickly.

Variation: Golden Beer Batter

¾   cup cornstarch
1   teaspoon salt
2⅔   cups flour
3   teaspoons sugar
⅛   teaspoon white pepper
1¾   cups water
2   egg yolks
⅓   cup flat beer
2   teaspoons baking powder

Combine dry ingredients, excluding the baking powder. In a separate bowl, combine the wet ingredients. Mix contents of the two bowls together. Fold in baking powder. Coat onions in batter, and fry as above.

Pink Adobe Potato Grande

YIELD: 6 SERVINGS

A recipe that is often asked for at the Pink Adobe is for the potato that we serve with steaks and shrimp. The preparation is very simple, with outstanding results. You must use *baking* potatoes to achieve the mealy texture that is the secret of this winner.

6	medium-size Idaho baking potatoes
4	quarts boiling water
	Cooking oil (enough to fill deep fryer 3 inches)
1	stick butter

Boil the unpeeled baking potatoes for 30–35 minutes. Test to see if they are done by inserting a fork into one potato. The fork should go through easily, but potato should remain firm. Pour off water and allow potatoes to cool. Peel potatoes. Heat oil in fryer to 400°F. Fry potatoes, only two or three at a time, until golden brown. Keep warm in 250°F oven until all are done. Cut a cross in one side of each potato and squeeze ends toward each other to pop the potato open. Press a generous pat of butter in opening of each potato. Serve hot.

Black-eyed Peas

YIELD: 6 SERVINGS

2	pounds fresh black-eyed peas, shelled
1	tablespoon minced onion
1	clove garlic, minced
1	large tomato, chopped
¼	cup bacon drippings
1	hot red pepper, crushed if dried, chopped if fresh

Chopped red onions
Freshly chopped green onions
Salsa Diabolique (page 22)
Green tomato relish
Green Chile Relish (page 19)

Cover peas with water in 2-quart saucepan and add remaining ingredients. Bring to a boil. Reduce heat and simmer for 1 hour or until peas are tender. Have small bowls of various garnishes on the table to please individual tastes.

Spaghetti Squash

YIELD: 6 SERVINGS

The most diverse of all in the large squash family is the spaghetti squash. It can be served with just butter, used in casseroles, seasoned and stuffed back into its own shell, used as a base for a sauce, or mixed with meat, fish, or other vegetables.

1   5-pound spaghetti squash

Pierce the skin in several places with a fork, then bake, boil, steam, or microwave, as explained below.

To bake: Preheat oven to 350°F. Place ½ inch of water in pan and add squash. Bake 1 hour or until shell is soft to touch.

To boil: Place in a 6-quart pan or roaster and boil 45 minutes to 1 hour, until shell gives when pressed.

To steam: Place in 6-quart pot containing 1 inch of boiling water. Cover. Check often to maintain constant water level. Steam for approximately 25–30 minutes.

To microwave: Set at high for 20 minutes, rotating squash every 5 minutes.

Whatever method you use, cool squash for 10 minutes. Cut in half lengthwise. Discard seeds. With fork, pull out strands of squash.

Spaghetti Squash Spring Casserole

YIELD: 6 SERVINGS

1	5-pound spaghetti squash, cooked and pulled into strands (page 129)
3	tablespoons butter
¼	cup chopped onion
¼	cup diced red bell pepper
¼	cup diced green bell pepper
1	cup julienned smoked ham
1	cup snow peas
1½	cups Quick White Sauce (page 131)
½	cup bread crumbs
1	cup freshly grated Parmesan cheese
	Freshly ground black pepper to taste

Preheat oven to 350°F. Place spaghetti squash strands in large bowl and set aside. Melt butter in 10-inch skillet. Sauté onion, peppers, and ham for 2 minutes. Add snow peas and sauté for 2 more minutes. Mix with squash and stir in white sauce. Place in buttered 2-quart casserole dish. Sprinkle with bread crumbs. Bake for 20 minutes. Serve with Parmesan cheese and freshly ground black pepper.

Southwestern Succotash

YIELD: 6 SERVINGS

Though you may be tempted to opt for the frozen lima beans and corn to save time, you really should try this with fresh vegetables. The difference in taste is well worth the effort.

    1   tablespoon bacon drippings
    1   tablespoon butter
    ½   cup chopped onion
    1   whole green chile, roasted, peeled, and chopped (page
         xiv)
    1   small red bell pepper, chopped
    ½   cup chopped pecans
    ½   cup canned condensed beef bouillon
         Dash Worcestershire sauce
    ½   teaspoon cayenne pepper
    ½   teaspoon salt
    2   cups cooked shelled fresh lima beans or 1 9-ounce pack-
         age frozen baby lima beans, cooked as directed on package
         Kernels scraped from 4 ears fresh corn on the cob (ap-
         proximately 2 cups) or 1 9-ounce package frozen whole
         kernel corn, cooked as directed on package
    ½   cup bread crumbs
    1   cup grated Monterey Jack cheese

Preheat oven to 350°F. Heat bacon drippings and butter in heavy
12-inch skillet. Add onions, green chile, red pepper, and pecans
and stir until onions are wilted. Add beef broth, Worcestershire,
cayenne, and salt. Add beans and corn. Stir to combine well.
Pour into well-buttered 1½-quart casserole. Sprinkle with bread
crumbs, then cheese. Bake for 35 minutes.

Quick White Sauce

YIELD: APPROXIMATELY 1½ CUPS

This recipe works only with instant flour. Do not use regular
flour, or you will get lumps.

    1   cup cold milk
    2   tablespoons Wondra flour (instant flour)
    2   tablespoons butter
    ¼   teaspoon salt
    ⅛   teaspoon freshly ground white pepper

Combine all ingredients in 1-quart saucepan. Heat until boiling,
stirring constantly. Cook about 1 minute.

Southwestern Vegetable Clafouti

YIELD: 6 SERVINGS

Although clafouti is a cobblerlike dessert, usually prepared with sweet cherries and baked in a large skillet in the oven, it can be made with a great variety of vegetables and served with a meat course. Try it with a combination of precooked diced seasoned vegetables of your choice.

2 cups diced cooked vegetables (see Note)
1 fresh jalapeño or serrano pepper, chopped, or 1 4-ounce can chopped green chiles, drained
Butter, salt, and pepper to taste

Batter

3 tablespoons melted butter
3 eggs
1 egg yolk
1½ cups milk
¾ cup flour
1 teaspoon sugar
½ teaspoon each salt and freshly ground black pepper

Preheat oven to 350°F. Mix vegetables and peppers and season with butter, salt, and pepper to taste. Place all batter ingredients in bowl of food processor or blender. Process until well blended. Butter a 3-quart sauté pan and pour half the batter into it. Cover with vegetables and add remaining batter. Bake for 45 minutes or until browned and puffed.

NOTE: Suggestions for vegetable combinations:
1. 1 cup cut green beans and 1 cup sautéed mushrooms
2. 1 cup peas and 1 cup carrots
3. 1 cup diced zucchini and 1 cup diced yellow summer squash
4. 1 cup corn and 1 cup lima beans
5. 1 package frozen mixed vegetables

Orange-Flavored Yams with Praline Topping

YIELD: 12 SERVINGS

Served as an accompaniment to the holiday turkey or with pork or chicken, there is no equal to this method of preparing yams.

2	40-ounce cans yams, drained (see Note)
¼	cup brandy
⅔	cup fresh orange juice
1	tablespoon grated orange rind
1	teaspoon salt
½	cup brown sugar
½	teaspoon ground ginger
¼	teaspoon freshly ground black pepper
3	egg yolks

Praline Topping

⅔	cup brown sugar
1½	cups chopped pecans
½	teaspoon ground cinnamon
½	cup butter, melted

Preheat oven to 350°F. Butter a 12-by-9-by-2-inch baking pan. Mash yams until smooth. Add brandy, orange juice, orange rind, salt, sugar, ginger, pepper; and egg yolks. Mix well and spoon into prepared dish. Mix topping ingredients together thoroughly. With a rubber spatula, spread evenly over yams. Bake 45–60 minutes, until brown and bubbly.

NOTE: This is one of the few instances where I prefer to use a canned vegetable. While you can of course make this recipe with fresh yams, it is very time-consuming, and especially tough during the busy holiday season.

Zucchini with Corn and Green Chiles

YIELD: 6 SERVINGS

¼ cup butter
1 tablespoon olive oil
½ cup chopped onion
½ cup chopped fresh green chiles
4 cups sliced zucchini (½ inch thick)
1½–2 cups fresh corn kernels (scraped from about 4 ears)
1 teaspoon salt
¼ teaspoon dried oregano
¼ teaspoon cumin seed
½ cup chicken or beef broth

Heat butter and olive oil in 12-inch skillet. Sauté onion and green chile for about 3 minutes. Add zucchini, corn, salt, oregano, and cumin seed. Stir and mix well. Add broth. Cover skillet and simmer until zucchini is crisp-tender, about 5 minutes.

Breads, Pasta, and Grains

Sunday morning treats, midnight snacks
—casseroles and rice dishes, plain rice—
Italian Risotto—Brown Rice and Wild
Rice. Various corn breads—spoon breads,
southwestern soufflés and unusual pasta
dishes.

Sweet and Savory Breads

Creole Calas

YIELD: 6 SERVINGS

This dish goes back to a time long before mine in New Orleans. These cakes were sold in the early morning hours by black women vendors. The cala women, as they were known, carrying covered bowls on their turbaned heads, would go through the streets chanting, "Belle cala! Tout chaud!" This was the signal for cooks to rush through the old patios to buy the hot fresh calas, which they carried to their masters and mistresses along with steaming chicory coffee.

½   cup rice
½   teaspoon butter
½   teaspoon salt
2   cups water
1   package (1 tablespoon) dry yeast
3   eggs, well beaten
¼   cup sugar
¼   teaspoon ground nutmeg
1¼ cups flour
    Pinch salt
    Vegetable oil for deep frying
    Powdered sugar

In a heavy 3-quart saucepan, combine the rice, butter, ½ teaspoon salt, and water. Bring to a boil. Lower heat to a simmer, cover pan tightly, and cook for 25 minutes. Drain rice in a colander. Place in a large deep bowl and mash into a mush. Add yeast and beat thoroughly. Set bowl in a warm place, cover with a towel, and let rise overnight. The next morning, add eggs, sugar, nutmeg, flour, and a pinch of salt. Beat until well mixed. Again, cover bowl, set in warm place, and let rise for 15–20 minutes. Heat oil in deep fryer to 350°F. Drop batter by tablespoons into hot oil and fry until golden brown, about 3–4 minutes. Cook only 3–4 at a time. Keep cooked calas on a platter in a warm oven until all are fried. Sprinkle with powdered sugar and serve hot.

Corn Tortillas

YIELD: 14 TO 16 TORTILLAS

While yellow and, with increasing frequency, blue corn tortillas are easily purchased at most supermarkets, there is a certain satisfaction in making one's own. A tortilla press helps considerably; these can be found in houseware departments or in Hispanic markets. You must use flour that is comprised of corn treated with lime and specially ground corn flour "masa." But this, too, is easily solved with a product of the Quaker company called "Masa Harina," an instant masa mix. All you have to do is add water.

2   cups Quaker Masa Harina
1   cup plus 2 tablespoons water

Combine Masa Harina with water and mix until the dough forms a ball. Add a teaspoon or two of additional water if necessary. Tear into pieces and form 14 to 16 balls. Cover with moist towel. Place 1 ball between 2 sheets of plastic wrap in tortilla press and press to form 6-inch circle. Carefully peel off plastic wrap. Bake on very hot (450°) ungreased griddle or heavy skillet for 30 seconds. Flip and continue cooking one minute. Flip again, cook for another 15–30 seconds. Once cooked, the tortillas should be soft and pliable.

Crêpes Maison Murphy

YIELD: 6 SERVINGS

After trying many recipes for crêpes and never being too satis-
fied, I have finally created a formula for a never-fail, very acceptable crêpe. And by using instant flour, you don't need to let the
batter rest for two hours before making the crêpes. This batter
can be used immediately after mixing.

Crêpe Batter

1½	cups instant flour
¾	cup cold milk
¾	cup cold water
3	large eggs
2	teaspoons melted butter
½	teaspoon salt
1	capful rum extract

Sauce

4	tablespoons butter
2	teaspoons chopped shallot
3	tablespoons flour
⅛	teaspoon ground nutmeg
	Dash ground cloves
	Few grains cayenne pepper
	Salt and white pepper to taste
2	cups chicken broth, warmed
½	cup diced Swiss cheese
1	8-ounce can evaporated milk, warmed

Filling

1½	cups chopped cooked chicken
1½	cups chopped cooked shrimp
3–4	teaspoons butter, melted, for glazing
¼	cup chopped fresh parsley, for garnish

Preheat oven to 375°F. With an electric hand mixer or wire whisk, beat all crêpe batter ingredients together until smooth. Lightly grease a 6-inch crêpe pan and heat it to approximately 375°F. Remove from heat and, holding the pan handle in one hand, pour in with the other hand just enough batter to barely cover bottom of pan as you tilt it in all directions. Return to heat and cook about a minute, until crêpe shakes loose. Either turn with a spatula or flip. (Flipping gives one a great feeling of achievement and is surprisingly simple with a little practice.) Cook on this side not quite a minute. Continue in this manner until all batter is used (12 crêpes), buttering pan when necessary.

Set aside crêpes, keeping them warm.

Prepare sauce: Melt butter in heavy 2-quart saucepan. Add shallot and sauté for 1–2 minutes. Stir in flour, nutmeg, cloves, cayenne pepper, and salt and white pepper to taste. Slowly add the warmed chicken broth, stirring constantly. Add cheese and, when it begins to melt, slowly add milk. Stir until smooth.

Combine chicken and shrimp in a bowl, then mix in half of the sauce. Put a large spoonful of this mixture on each crêpe and roll the crêpes loosely. Place crêpes close together in a buttered 12-by-9-by-2-inch baking dish. Spoon remaining sauce over top of each, distributing sauce evenly. Bake 15 minutes, then brown under broiler for about 2 minutes. Glaze with a few teaspoons of melted butter. Garnish with chopped parsley.

Flour Tortillas

YIELD: 12 TORTILLAS

You can buy fresh tortillas in most supermarkets these days, but there's nothing like the ones you make at home and serve instantly. Use these to make Tostados (page 3) or to serve with any dinner. You can also freeze them, wrapped in plastic wrap, for later use.

- 2 cups flour
- ½ teaspoon salt
- ¼ cup lard
- ½ cup warm water
- ¼ cup vegetable oil

In a medium bowl, combine flour and salt. With fingers, work in lard until evenly mixed. Gradually add water to make a soft dough. Divide dough in half. Then divide halves into three parts and each third in half to make 12 pieces of dough. Form each into a ball. Dip fingers into vegetable oil and coat each ball with oil. Cover balls with cloth and let stand 10–15 minutes. Lightly flour a flat surface and, with a floured rolling pin, roll each ball into a large circle, about 8 inches in diameter. Place on a hot, ungreased griddle, and when bubbles appear on top, turn tortillas to cook other side. Tortillas should be flecked with brown spots but still soft and tender. Serve immediately.

Michelle Naranjo's Indian Bread

YIELD: 2 LOAVES

One day recently a group of friends and I were invited to visit the Santa Clara Pueblo, which is about 25 miles from Santa Fe, to observe bread baking in the ancient Indian manner. The outside oven that is used is called an *horno* (pronounced *or-no*). It is made of adobe, shaped like a beehive, and deep enough to hold 25 loaves of bread. The oven that was used that day had been in service for 35 years. To prepare the oven for baking, many logs are placed on the hearth and allowed to burn until they are amber in color and almost ashes. The log pieces are then removed, and the horno is quickly cleaned out with a wet mop. The unbaked bread is put into the oven with a long wooden paddle, and the front opening is then sealed with a large, square piece of plywood. The bread is baked for one hour.

7   cups flour
½   teaspoon salt
⅓   cup lard
1   teaspoon active dry yeast
1½ cups lukewarm water
½   teaspoon sugar

Preheat oven to 350°F. In a large bowl, combine the flour and salt, then cut in the lard until mixture is crumbly. In a separate, smaller bowl, combine the yeast, water, and sugar. Set aside yeast mixture until the yeast and sugar are dissolved and the mixture is foamy. When foamy, mix into the flour-lard mixture. Knead until dough is pliable and has an elastic consistency, about 7 minutes. Place dough in a greased bowl, cover, and allow to rise in a warm, draft-free place until doubled (about 4 hours). Punch down dough and divide in half. Shape the dough into two circular loaves and place them on an ungreased baking sheet (or place each loaf in a medium-size bread pan). Cover the loaves and let rise again in a warm, draft-free place for another 2 hours. Bake for 45–60 minutes or until the bottom of each loaf sounds hollow when tapped. Cool 10 minutes and turn out onto rack.

Jalapeño Corn Bread

YIELD: 12 SERVINGS

2½ cups yellow cornmeal
1 cup flour
2 tablespoons sugar
1 tablespoon salt
4 teaspoons baking powder
½ cup nonfat dry milk
3 eggs, room temperature
1½ cups warm water
½ cup cooking oil
1 17-ounce can cream-style corn
6–8 jalapeño peppers, chopped
2 cups grated sharp cheddar cheese
1 large onion, grated
2–3 slices bacon, cooked and crumbled (optional)

Preheat oven to 425°F. Stir dry ingredients together. In a smaller, separate bowl, beat eggs lightly, then stir in water and oil. Pour the liquid mixture into cornmeal mixture. Stir in the creamed corn, jalapeños, cheese, onion, and bacon. In two greased 9-by-11-inch or 9-inch-square glass pans, bake mixture for 30 minutes. (Do not use metal pans for baking or wrap this bread in aluminum foil as the acid in the jalapeños will leach the foil.) Serve warm.

Sopapillas (Fried Bread)

YIELD: APPROXIMATELY 4 DOZEN

Throughout Mexico and New Mexico, sopapillas are a traditional substitute for bread at the dinner table. These are delicious golden fried puffs—crisp and lightly browned on the outside, hollow on the inside. Sopapillas are usually served with honey and are equally delicious stuffed with chili con carne and beans.

4   cups flour
4   teaspoons baking powder
1   teaspoon salt
3   tablespoons lard
¾   cup warm water
    Oil for deep frying

Into a large bowl sift together flour, baking powder, and salt. Cut in lard and mix with hands until mixture resembles cornmeal. Stir in warm water to make a dry dough. Knead until smooth, about 5 minutes. Cover dough with plastic wrap and let stand for 30 minutes. Roll out dough about ¼ inch thick on a lightly floured surface. Cut into 3-inch squares. Pour oil about 3 inches deep into a deep fryer and heat to 400°F. Carefully drop dough squares a few at a time into hot oil. They will puff immediately. Turn to brown other side, then drain on paper towels. Serve at once.

New Mexican Spoon Bread

YIELD: 6 SERVINGS

1   17-ounce can cream-style corn
¾   cup milk
⅓   cup melted shortening
1½   cups white cornmeal
2   eggs, slightly beaten
½   teaspoon baking soda
1   teaspoon baking powder
1   teaspoon salt
½   cup roasted, peeled, and chopped fresh green chiles (page xiv) or 1 4-ounce can green chiles, drained and chopped
1½   cups grated Monterey Jack cheese

Preheat oven to 375°F. In a large bowl, combine all ingredients except chiles and cheese. Pour one half of the batter into a greased 9-inch-square pan. Sprinkle half of the chiles and half of the cheese onto the batter. Add remaining batter and top with remaining chiles and cheese. Bake for 45 minutes, until firm around the edges and slightly soft in the center. Spoon from pan onto plates.

Pasta and Grains

Fettuccine with Green Chile-Anchovy Sauce

YIELD: 6 SERVINGS

Check the index for other pasta dishes. For example, Lasagna Monte can be found in the poultry chapter and Linguine with Oysters and Green Chiles in the seafood chapter.

1   1-pound package spinach fettuccine
¾   cup olive oil
1   cup thinly sliced fresh green chiles, roasted and peeled (page xiv)
¼   cup thinly sliced red bell pepper
⅓   cup piñons (pine nuts)
1   2-ounce can anchovy fillets
1   cup grated Parmesan cheese
    Salt and freshly ground black pepper to taste

Cook pasta to al dente stage according to package directions. Heat olive oil in 10-inch skillet. Sauté chiles, red pepper, piñons, and anchovies, stirring gently and mashing anchovies lightly until heated through. Add cheese, salt, and pepper. Stir well and mix with hot cooked pasta.

Pink Adobe Spaghetti I

YIELD: 6 SERVINGS

2	cloves garlic, minced
1	medium onion, chopped
1	medium bell pepper, chopped
3	stalks celery, chopped
1	small carrot, chopped
½	cup finely chopped fresh parsley
¼	cup olive oil
1	pound lean ground beef
½	pound ground pork
1	teaspoon chili powder
	Salt to taste
1	24-ounce can crushed tomatoes
2	6-ounce cans tomato paste
1	pinch each dried oregano, cumin seeds, dried basil, dried rosemary, dried thyme, and dried marjoram
1	bay leaf
1	pound fresh mushrooms, sliced
½	cup red wine
1	pound spaghetti, cooked
1	cup grated Parmesan cheese
1	6-ounce can pitted black olives, for garnish
	Additional chopped fresh parsley, for garnish

Sauté the garlic and fresh vegetables in olive oil until soft but not brown. Add the meats, chili powder, and salt to taste. Mix well and cook until the meat browns. Add tomatoes, paste, herbs, and sliced mushrooms. Cover and simmer slowly for 1 hour, adding red wine as needed to keep sauce from getting too thick; stir occasionally. Pour over freshly cooked spaghetti, cover with cheese, and garnish with the ripe olives and more chopped parsley.

Pink Adobe Spaghetti II

YIELD: 6 SERVINGS

This is a very potent sauce; a little goes a long way. We always serve this spaghetti with meatballs (recipe follows).

- ¼ pound butter
- ½ clove garlic
- 2 tablespoons chopped fresh parsley
- 1 tablespoon chopped fresh basil *or* 1 teaspoon dried basil
- ¼ cup olive oil
- 1 pound spaghetti, cooked

In a 12-inch skillet, melt the butter and press the garlic into it. Add the parsley and basil. Cook for 5 minutes over moderate heat, stirring constantly. Do not allow butter to boil. Remove from heat and add olive oil. Chill to harden. Serve with hot spaghetti, letting diners help themselves to the chilled sauce.

Meatballs

YIELD: 6 SERVINGS

- 1 medium onion, chopped
- 3 tablespoons butter
- 1½ pounds ground top round
- 1 pint sour cream
- 1 pinch Fine Herbes
- ½ teaspoon salt
- ¼ teaspoon pepper

In medium skillet, sauté the onion in 1 tablespoon of the butter. Remove onion, reserve the butter. Mix onion with the meat, half the cream, herbs, and salt and pepper. Form into 12 balls. Add remaining butter to skillet, and sauté meatballs in this. Remove meatballs from pan. Add rest of sour cream to pan. Scrape pan well and cook cream and scrapings into a light gravy. Pour over meatballs and serve.

Red Beans and Rice

YIELD: 6 SERVINGS

4	cups dry red beans
2	tablespoons bacon fat
1	medium onion, chopped
2	cups (16 ounces) canned tomato sauce
1	teaspoon salt
½	teaspoon freshly ground black pepper
1	tablespoon vinegar
1	teaspoon Tabasco sauce
1	teaspoon crushed red pepper flakes
¼	teaspoon dried thyme
1½–2	pounds meaty ham hock
3	cups cooked white rice
¼	cup chopped onion, for garnish
	Few drops Tabasco sauce, for garnish
½	pound sausage, cooked and sliced, for garnish

Clean and wash beans. Soak in large pot overnight. When ready to cook, drain off water. In a heavy 4-quart pot or Dutch oven, heat the bacon fat. Sauté onions until wilted. Add the beans, tomato sauce, salt, pepper, vinegar, Tabasco, red pepper, and thyme. Add enough water to cover beans. Simmer until beans are semicooked, about 30 minutes. Remove 1 cup of beans and drain. Mash in processor or blender. Return mashed beans to pot along with ham hock and cook over low heat for 2 hours, until the mixture is creamy, stirring occasionally. (The beans should be creamy and juicy. Toward the end of cooking time, if the beans seem to dry, add a little broth or tomato juice.) When done, remove ham hock. Remove meat from hock and return meat to the pot. Stir to mix. Evenly divide the rice into 6 individual serving bowls. Spoon the beans over rice. Garnish with chopped onion, Tabasco sauce, and cooked sausage slices. Serve hot French bread on the side.

Black Beans and Rice Alvarez

YIELD: 6–8 SERVINGS

2	cups dry black beans
10	cups water
2	medium green bell peppers, chopped fine
1	cup plus 2 tablespoons olive oil
1	large onion, chopped fine
2	cloves garlic, minced
2	teaspoons salt
½	teaspoon freshly ground black pepper
¼	teaspoon dried oregano
1	bay leaf
1	tablespoon sugar
2	tablespoons vinegar
2	tablespoons dry vermouth
4	cups cooked white rice

Wash beans and soak in water with one of the chopped bell peppers overnight. Do not drain. Cook beans in the same water for 45 minutes.

Heat 1 cup of the olive oil in a 12-inch skillet and lightly sauté onion, garlic, and the other chopped bell pepper. Remove 1 cup of the cooked beans from pot, mash well in food processor or blender, and add to vegetables in skillet. Mix, then add skillet mixture to remaining beans. Add salt, pepper, oregano, bay leaf, and sugar. Cover and simmer over low heat for 1 hour. Add vinegar and vermouth and simmer over low heat for another hour. If beans are watery at the end of this time, remove cover and cook over a higher heat a little longer, until thickened but still creamy. Just before serving, add the remaining 2 tablespoons of olive oil. Serve over boiled white rice.

Priscilla's Perfect Tamales

YIELD: 24 TAMALES

These are cocktail-size tamales, the perfect finger food for an informal party.

Filling

1	cup grated cheddar cheese
1	cup grated Swiss cheese
¼	cup chopped black olives
⅛	cup chopped piñons (pine nuts)
½	cup minced onion
1	clove garlic, minced
1	tablespoon dried oregano
1	teaspoon ground cumin
1	cup cooked fresh corn kernels (scraped from about 2 ears) or 1 8-ounce can whole kernel corn, drained
½	cup roasted, peeled, and chopped fresh green chiles (page xiv) or 1 4-ounce can green chiles, chopped
1	teaspoon olive oil

Masa

1	29-ounce can hominy, drained
	Dash salt
	Dash Tabasco sauce
1	8-ounce package corn husks, soaked in warm water

In large bowl, combine all filling ingredients and set aside.

In food processor fitted with steel blade, process hominy until smooth. Season with salt and Tabasco. Spread husks out and spread each with 1½ tablespoons of the masa. Then place 1–1½ tablespoons of filling on each, spreading evenly. Roll husks up like cigarettes and, halfway through rolling, tuck tip and bottom ends in, then continue to roll completely. Steam for 45 minutes. (An easy method of steaming is to place a colander into a large soup pot with 1 inch of boiling water. Cover to steam.) Serve hot.

New Mexican Spanish Rice

YIELD: 6 SERVINGS

3	slices lean bacon
1	cup long-grain white rice
1	8-ounce can tomatoes, crushed, with liquid
½	cup chopped onion
¼	cup sliced pitted black olives
½	cup chopped green bell pepper
½	cup roasted, peeled, and chopped fresh green chiles (page xiv) or 1 4-ounce can green chiles, chopped
1	teaspoon salt
1	teaspoon chili powder
1	10¾-ounce can chicken broth
1	6-ounce can Snappy Tom (Bloody Mary mix)
2	tablespoons olive oil
2	tablespoons chopped cilantro, for garnish

In a heavy 2-quart pot, fry bacon until crisp. Remove bacon from pan, crumble, and reserve. Fry rice in bacon drippings until brown, stirring constantly. Add tomatoes, onion, olives, bell pepper, green chiles, salt, and chili powder. Mix well. Add chicken broth and Snappy Tom, cover, and cook until liquid is absorbed, 30–45 minutes. Transfer to serving bowl and, just before serving, sprinkle with olive oil. Garnish with cilantro.

Brown Rice with Fresh Pears

YIELD: 6 SERVINGS

This is wonderful served for breakfast. It is also great served with Garden of Eden Pork Roast (page 107).

2   tablespoons butter
½   cup chopped onion
½   cup chopped green bell pepper
1½ cups brown rice
¼   teaspoon freshly ground black pepper
2½ cups chicken broth
2   ripe pears, cored and sliced thin
½   cup pecan pieces
2   tablespoons chopped fresh parsley

Melt butter in heavy 2-quart pot. Add onion and green pepper and sauté lightly. Add rice and black pepper and sauté for 1–2 minutes more, stirring constantly. Add chicken broth. Cover and simmer for 45–60 minutes, until rice is tender and liquid is absorbed. Mix in pears, pecans, and parsley. Stir gently to distribute evenly.

Grits Soufflé

YIELD: 6 SERVINGS

This down-home dish can take the place of potatoes or rice at any meal.

2   cups cooked creamy grits
6   tablespoons soft butter
3   egg yolks
½   teaspoon freshly ground black pepper
½   pound sharp cheddar cheese, grated
6   egg whites
     Pinch cream of tartar

Preheat oven to 450°F. Butter a 2-quart soufflé dish. When grits are cooked (according to package directions), remove from heat and stir in butter, egg yolks, pepper, and half the cheddar cheese. Set aside. Beat egg whites with cream of tartar. Fold into grits mixture with a rubber spatula; use a light rolling motion until all egg whites are incorporated. Pour into prepared soufflé dish, top with remaining cheese, and bake 35–40 minutes, until set.

Sausage and Wild Rice Casserole

YIELD: 6 SERVINGS

1	pound sausage meat
1	pound mushrooms, sliced
1	cup chopped onions
¼	cup flour
½	cup heavy cream
2	10-ounce cans chicken broth
2	cups cooked and drained wild rice
1	pinch dried oregano
1	pinch dried thyme
1	pinch dried marjoram
1	teaspoon salt
	Freshly ground black pepper and Tabasco sauce to taste
½	cup slivered blanched almonds for garnish

Preheat oven to 350°F. Sauté the sausage meat until all the fat has cooked out into the pan. Remove meat and break into small pieces. Set aside and keep warm. Sauté mushrooms and onions in the fat and return sausage meat. Put flour and cream into a small mixing bowl and mix until there are no lumps. Add to meat and vegetables. Stir, add the chicken broth, and cook until thickened to the consistency of a thick soup. Add the cooked rice, herbs, and seasonings. Transfer to a buttered 2-quart casserole dish and bake for 25–30 minutes. Sprinkle with the almonds and serve.

Green Chile Risotto

YIELD: 6 SERVINGS

5	cups chicken broth
2	tablespoons butter
2	tablespoons olive oil
½	cup minced onion
2	cups Italian Arborio rice, *well washed*
⅓	cup vermouth
½	cup roasted, peeled, and chopped fresh green chiles (page xiv) *or* 1 4-ounce can hot green chiles, chopped
⅔	cup grated Parmesan cheese
½	teaspoon white pepper

In a 2-quart saucepan, bring chicken broth to a simmer. Keep broth hot while heating butter and oil over low heat in a 3-quart saucepan. Add onion to butter and oil and sauté until limp. Add rice, stirring with a wooden spoon, until the rice is well coated with the butter and oil. Add vermouth, stirring until wine is absorbed. Then add about ⅔ cup of the simmering broth, stirring until it is absorbed. Continue in this manner, adding about ⅔ cup of broth at a time until all is used and rice is al dente. This procedure takes almost 30 minutes. Remove pan from heat and stir in chiles, Parmesan cheese, and pepper. Serve hot.

Desserts

In my opinion, fresh pears and a sharp cheese are the happiest and tastiest conclusions to a pleasurable dinner. But for those with a fancy for the sweeter things of life in a more elaborate form, here are a few that will delight both the eye and the palate.

French Apple Pie

YIELD: 6 SERVINGS

This is the favorite dessert at the Pink Adobe. I have no idea how many French Apple Pies I've made—thousands, hundreds of thousands, maybe millions. At any rate, they've all been eaten with gusto.

Crust

    2   cups flour
    ¾   cup lard
    1   teaspoon salt
    6–7 tablespoons cold water

Filling

    1   pound fresh or 1 16-ounce can apples, peeled and sliced
    2   tablespoons fresh lemon juice
    ½   teaspoon ground nutmeg
    ½   teaspoon ground cinnamon
    ½   cup white sugar
    ¼   cup seedless raisins
    1   cup brown sugar
    2   tablespoons flour
    2   tablespoons butter
    ½   cup shelled pecans
    ¼   cup milk

Hard Sauce

    ½   cup butter
    1½   cups powdered sugar
    1   tablespoon boiling water
    1   teaspoon brandy or rum

Preheat oven to 450°F. Prepare the crust: Work the flour, lard, and salt together with your fingers until crumbly. Add water until dough holds together. Divide into 2 equal balls. On a floured pastry cloth, roll out one ball thin enough to line a 9-inch pie tin. Roll out second ball in same manner for the top crust.

Prepare filling: Put the apples in the lined pie tin and sprinkle with lemon juice, nutmeg, and cinnamon. Spread white sugar and raisins evenly over apples. Mix the brown sugar, flour, and butter in a bowl; when well blended, spread over the contents of the pie tin and sprinkle with pecans. Add most of the milk and cover with the top crust. Prick top with a fork and brush the rest of the milk on the pastry. Bake for 10 minutes, then reduce heat to 350°F and bake another 30 minutes. Crust should be golden when done.

Hard Sauce: Cream the butter until light. Beat in the sugar and add water. Beat in liquor and serve on each slice of pie.

Flaming Sundae

I invented this recipe more than forty years ago and it was an instant success. My friends still talk about their first ones and insisted I include the recipe. I said I didn't think marshmallows have a place in this cookbook, but I was overruled. So here's a real treat for kids of all ages (be careful of the flame)!

1	scoop ice cream
2	tablespoons chocolate or butterscotch topping
1	sugar cube
1	teaspoon lemon extract
1	marshmallow

Place the scoop of ice cream in a serving bowl; top with topping. Soak sugar cube with lemon extract. Make a small (sugar-cube size) well in marshmallow. Push the soaked cube onto the marshmallow; push the marshmallow into the ice cream (if the ice cream is hard, you can first make a marshmallow-size well in the ice cream with a teaspoon). Tell everyone to stand back, light the sugar cube and impress!

Biscochitos

Y<small>IELD</small>: 3 <small>DOZEN</small>

This is a traditional New Mexican cookie.

2   cups lard
1   cup sugar
1   egg yolk
1   teaspoon aniseed
6   cups flour
1   teaspoon salt
2   teaspoons baking powder
½–¾ cup water
½   cup sugar, for topping
½   teaspoon ground cinnamon, for topping

Preheat oven to 350°F. In a large bowl, cream lard, 1 cup sugar, and egg yolk together until mixture is light and fluffy. Stir in aniseed. Sift together flour, salt, and baking powder and stir into creamed mixture. Stir in just enough water to make mixture hold together. Knead until well mixed. On a floured board, roll dough to ½-inch thickness. Cut into fancy shapes with cookie cutters. Mix together the ½ cup sugar and the cinnamon and sprinkle over each cookie. On an ungreased cookie sheet, bake for approximately 10 minutes, until nicely browned.

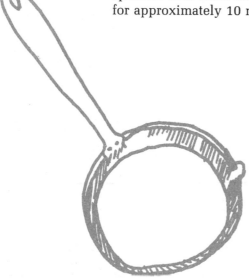

Southwestern Bread Pudding

YIELD: 8–10 SERVINGS

½	pound stale French bread
1	cup milk
¼	pound (1 stick) butter, melted
½	cup golden raisins
¼	cup piñons (pine nuts)
3	eggs, beaten
1¼	cups granulated sugar
¼	cup brown sugar
1	4-ounce can evaporated milk
1	8¼-ounce can crushed pineapple with juice
1	tablespoon fresh lemon juice
3	teaspoons vanilla
	Tequila Sauce (recipe follows)

Preheat oven to 350°F. Break bread into bite-size chunks; soak in milk. Squeeze bread with your fingers to eliminate excess liquid and discard milk. Set bread in a large bowl and add remaining ingredients except sauce. Very gently, mix thoroughly. Pour mixture into an 8-by-12-inch buttered baking pan. Bake for 1 hour or until a knife inserted in the center comes out clean. Serve with Tequila Sauce.

Tequila Sauce

YIELD: 1 CUP

1	cup granulated sugar
1	egg
¼	pound (1 stick) butter, melted
⅓	cup *good-quality* tequila (see Note)
1	teaspoon fresh lime juice

NOTE: Tequila may be replaced by rum, bourbon, Irish whiskey, or whiskey of your choice.

Cream sugar and egg together. Add butter and pour into a medium saucepan. Over a low flame, stir mixture until sugar is dissolved. Remove from heat and stir in tequila and lime juice. Pour over servings of Southwestern Bread Pudding.

Chocolate Denise

A delectable dessert named after a discerning granddaughter.

½   cup Madeira
6   ladyfingers, split in half
    Chocolate Pudding (page 161)
1   cup heavy cream
1   teaspoon orange extract
2   tablespoons piñons (pine nuts)

Place Madeira in shallow dish with sides. Dip ladyfingers in wine. Stand 2 halves of ladyfingers on the inside of each of 6 7-ounce long-stemmed wineglasses, then fill wineglasses with chocolate pudding. Let stand until set. Just before serving, whip cream with orange extract. Divide evenly among glasses. Sprinkle with piñons.

Chocolate Mousse

YIELD: 6–8 SERVINGS

4   squares (4 ounces) semisweet chocolate
½   package (2 ounces) German sweet chocolate
1   tablespoon strong black coffee
1   teaspoon instant espresso
¾   cup sugar
¼   cup water
4   eggs, separated
1   tablespoon butter
1   teaspoon rum or ½ teaspoon rum extract
1   cup whipping cream, whipped
    Grated orange peel, for garnish
    Grated semisweet chocolate, for garnish

Combine chocolates, coffee, and espresso and melt in top of double boiler. In separate saucepan, boil sugar and water until syrupy. Beat egg yolks. When chocolate is melted, stir in syrup and egg yolks. Mix well and remove from heat. *Do not cook.* Immediately add butter and rum. Place pan over bowl of ice to cool mixture. Beat egg whites until stiff. Beat cream until firm. With a rubber spatula, fold beaten egg whites into cooled chocolate mixture and then fold in whipped cream. Reserve a little of the whipped cream for garnish. Turn mousse into a lightly oiled 1½-quart mold or 6–8 individual serving glasses. Chill for several hours. Unmold mousse on plate or serve in glasses, garnished with whipped cream, grated orange peel, and/or grated chocolate.

Chocolate Pudding

YIELD: 6 SERVINGS

This pudding is delicious when spooned into ladyfinger-lined wineglasses, as in Chocolate Denise (page 160).

1	cup sugar
½	teaspoon salt
2	tablespoons cornstarch
2	squares (2 ounces) unsweetened chocolate
2	cups milk
2	egg yolks, slightly beaten
2	tablespoons unsalted butter, softened
1	teaspoon vanilla

Combine sugar, salt, cornstarch, chocolate, and milk in a heavy 2-quart saucepan or top of double boiler. Stir over low heat until chocolate melts and mixture thickens. Stir egg yolks into a small amount of the hot mixture in a separate bowl. Pour yolk mixture back into remaining hot mixture in the saucepan and cook for another 2–3 minutes, stirring constantly. Remove from heat. Add butter and vanilla and stir.

Lemon Meringue Pie

YIELD: 6 SERVINGS

Crust

1½ cups flour
⅔ cup lard
1 teaspoon salt
5–6 tablespoons cold water

Filling

1 cup sugar
½ cup cornstarch
¼ teaspoon salt
1½ cups boiling water
4 egg yolks
⅓ cup fresh lemon juice
2 tablespoons grated lemon peel
2 tablespoons butter

Meringue

4 egg whites
¼ teaspoon salt
¼ teaspoon cream of tartar
¼ cup sugar
½ teaspoon fresh lemon juice

Preheat oven to 375°F. Prepare crust: Work flour, lard, and 1 teaspoon salt together with your fingers until crumbly. Add cold water, working until dough holds together. Form into ball and chill slightly, about 15–20 minutes. Roll out on a floured pastry cloth into a circle 11 inches in diameter. Fit into a 9-inch pie tin and flute edges of crust. Place a piece of foil over uncooked crust. Weight down foil with about 2 cups of dry beans or rice (to prevent bubbling or flaking of crust) and bake for 10–15 minutes.

Remove beans and foil, reduce oven temperature to 325°F, and bake 3–4 more minutes. Cool before filling.

Prepare filling: In a 2-quart saucepan, thoroughly mix 1 cup sugar, cornstarch, and ¼ teaspoon salt. Gradually add boiling water, a little at a time. Stir until clear and mixture thickens, about 2 minutes. Remove from heat. Mix egg yolks with ⅓ cup lemon juice. Return clear mixture to low heat and gradually stir in egg-lemon mixture. Stir at a boil for 1 minute. Add lemon peel and butter. Pour into cooled pastry shell.

Prepare meringue: With electric beater, beat egg whites until frothy. Add ¼ teaspoon salt and cream of tartar. Beat in ¼ cup sugar, a tablespoon at a time, until meringue is stiff. Add ½ teaspoon lemon juice and beat again to distribute. Pile meringue on top of filling in shell, spreading to edges. Bake at 350°F for 15 minutes or until meringue appears slightly golden tan in color. Allow to cool thoroughly before serving.

Peaches in Port Wine

YIELD: 6 SERVINGS

1   pint port wine
3   large halved and prepared (see Note) fresh peaches, or 1 16-ounce can peach halves
1   quart vanilla ice cream

Pour about 1 inch of port wine into a tall narrow jar or ice tea glass. Into this slide 1 peach half and fill cavity with more port. Add another peach and more wine and continue until glass is filled and peaches are stacked. Refrigerate for 3–4 days. Transfer a peach half to each of dessert dishes and fill center of each with a scoop of vanilla ice cream.

NOTE: To prepare fresh peaches, drop in boiling water for about 30 seconds to loosen peel, remove from water, peel, halve, and pit. Poach in water, wine, or orange juice (just enough liquid to cover the peaches) about 3 minutes (until tender). Remove from poaching liquid and chill thoroughly.

Margarita Pie

YIELD: 6 SERVINGS

Crust

2   cups graham cracker crumbs
½   cup butter, melted

Filling

1   envelope (1 tablespoon) unflavored gelatin
½   cup fresh lime juice
4   large eggs, separated
1   cup sugar
¼   teaspoon salt
1   teaspoon grated lime rind
⅓   cup tequila
3   tablespoons Triple Sec

Topping

1   cup whipping cream
2   tablespoons sugar
1–2 limes, sliced thin, for garnish

Prepare crust: place graham cracker crumbs in food processor and process until fine. Mix in butter (do not process) and press into a 9-inch pie tin. Chill in refrigerator.

Prepare filling: Sprinkle gelatin over lime juice in a small bowl. Allow to soften. In the top of a double boiler, beat egg yolks. Add ½ cup of sugar, then stir in gelatin mixture. Stir constantly over boiling water until slightly thickened. Remove from heat. Add salt, lime rind, tequila, and Triple Sec. Beat with a whisk. Pour into a large mixing bowl and cover. Chill for 5 minutes. While this mixture is chilling, beat egg whites with remaining sugar until stiff (peaks will form when beater is lifted out of mixture). With a rubber spatula, fold into the chilled mixture. Pour into crust, cover, and chill overnight.

Before serving, make topping: Beat cream. Add 2 tablespoons sugar and beat until thickened. Spread over top of pie. Garnish with lime slices.

Easy Chocolate Cake

YIELD: 6–8 SERVINGS

Very easy, very Creole, and always successful.

    1   cup dairy sour cream
    1½   cups sugar
    ¼   cup milk
    2   cups flour
    ¼   teaspoon salt
    1   teaspoon baking soda
    2   eggs, beaten
    4   squares (4 ounces) unsweetened chocolate
    ½   cup hot water

Icing

    1   8-ounce package cream cheese
    2   squares (2 ounces) unsweetened chocolate
    ⅛   cup milk
    ¾–1 cup powdered sugar
    1   cup pecan halves

Preheat oven to 350°F. Mix sour cream, 1½ cups sugar, and milk in a large bowl. Sift in flour, salt, and baking soda. Stir in the eggs. Melt the chocolate in water and stir into the flour mixture. Pour into a greased and floured 8½-by-14-inch oblong pan. Bake for 40 minutes or until a straw comes out from center clean. Let cool until sides shrink from pan (about 10 minutes).

Prepare icing: Mash the cream cheese until soft. Melt chocolate in milk over low heat. Mix with cream cheese and add enough powdered sugar to thicken the icing. Spread over entire cake with a knife and cover top and sides with pecan halves.

Pecan Pie

Filling

- 1   cup sugar
- 1   tablespoon butter
- 3   eggs
- 1   cup white corn syrup
- 2   cups pecan halves

Crust

- 1   cup flour
- 6   tablespoons lard
- ½   teaspoon salt
- 3–4 tablespoons cold water

Preheat oven to 350°F. Prepare the filling: Cream the sugar, butter, and eggs together. Add the syrup and pecans.

Prepare the crust: Work the flour, lard, and salt together with your fingers until crumbly. Add water until dough holds together. On a floured pastry cloth, roll out dough thin enough to line a 9-inch pie tin. Line tin with dough and crimp edges. Add pecan filling and bake about 30 minutes, until set.

Pralines

YIELD: APPROXIMATELY 15 PRALINES

- 1½ cups brown sugar
- ¼   cup (scant) milk or cream
- 2   tablespoons butter
- 1   cup shelled pecans

Put the sugar and milk in a 2-quart saucepan and stir continuously over low heat until mixture reaches thread stage. Then add the butter and pecans and cook until syrup forms a soft ball in cold water (drop a very small amount in cold water). Remove from flame. Cool for a few minutes without stirring, then beat until slightly thickened. Drop by teaspoonfuls onto a buttered cookie sheet and cool until hardened.

Pears Amaretto

YIELD: 6 SERVINGS

- 3 ounces Amaretto
- 1 16-ounce can pear halves
  Vanilla Custard (page 169)
- 1 cup heavy cream, whipped
  Sliced almonds, for garnish

Pour ½ ounce (1 tablespoon) Amaretto into each of 6 7-ounce wineglasses. Place one pear half in each glass, cut side up. Top each pear with vanilla custard. Cover each with a generous dollop of whipped cream. Sprinkle sliced almonds on top.

Strawberries with Champagne

YIELD: 6 SERVINGS

- 1 teaspoon fresh lemon juice
  Sugar to taste
- 2 tablespoons Cointreau
- 1 quart fresh strawberries
- 1 split champagne

Add lemon juice, sugar to taste (depends on sweetness of berries), and Cointreau to the strawberries in large mixing bowl. Pour champagne over strawberries and serve at once.

Sicilian Cake

YIELD: 6 TO 8 SERVINGS

1 frozen pound cake, about 9 inches long

Filling

1	pound ricotta cheese
1	cup sugar
1	cup mixed candied fruit, chopped coarse
2	ounces German chocolate, chopped
½	ounce Strega liqueur

Frosting

2	8-ounce squares German chocolate
¼	cup black coffee
1	tablespoon instant espresso
½	ounce Strega liqueur
¾	pound unsalted butter, cut into small pieces

Allow pound cake to thaw partially.

While thawing, prepare filling: Beat cheese until smooth. Fold in other filling ingredients.

With a sharp knife, remove the brown crust from the sides and top of cake. Slice horizontally into at least 6 slices. Place one slab of cake on bottom of a cake plate and spread generously with filling mixture. Place another slab on top and repeat with more filling. Continue this process until filling and cake slices are used, ending with a plain slice of cake on top. Gently shape loaf with hands. Refrigerate for 1–2 hours.

While cake is chilling, prepare frosting: Melt chocolate with the coffees in a double boiler, stirring constantly. Remove from heat. Add Strega liqueur and butter and beat until smooth. Chill mixture until it thickens to spreading consistency. With a spatula, spread frosting over sides and top of cake in decorative swirls. Chill overnight.

Vanilla Custard

YIELD: 6 SERVINGS

    1½ cups milk
    ½ cup sugar
    ¼ cup flour
    4   egg yolks, well beaten
    1   teaspoon vanilla

Scald milk and set aside. In top of double boiler over hot water, blend sugar, flour, and yolks. Cream mixture until light. Gradually add scalded milk. Stir until well blended. Cook, stirring constantly, until it reaches a boil and coats spoon. Remove from heat. Add vanilla and stir well. Cover tightly with waxed paper. Cool thoroughly.

Beverages

These beverage recipes have brought fame and approval to the Pink Adobe's Dragon Room bar. Most are fiery in character, with a definite southwestern flavor.

Brandy Freeze

YIELD: 1 SERVING

1   ounce brandy
1   ounce dark crème de cacao
1   scoop (4 ounces) jamoca ice cream
1   handful (approximately 4 ounces) ice

In a blender, mix all ingredients until thick. Sprinkle grated chocolate on top. Serve in a 12-ounce brandy snifter.

Sangrita

YIELD: 1 QUART

This drink is delicious served as a chaser to tequila—a jigger of Sangrita to a jigger of tequila.

2½ cups tomato juice
1   cup orange juice
¼   cup lime juice
1   tablespoon chopped seeded serrano chile or jalapeño pepper
2–3 ice cubes
2   tablespoons chopped onion

Combine all ingredients in a blender and puree.

Variation: Sangrita Cocktail

YIELD: 1 SERVING

Mix together 1½ ounces of vodka to 3 ounces of Sangrita. Serve in cocktail glass over ice and garnish with lime.

Creole Mary

While the garnishes may appear extravagant, don't hesitate to use them all—only the lime is optional!

- 1½ ounces Russian vodka
- 4 ounces tomato juice
  Dash Rose's lime juice
  Dash Worcestershire sauce
  Dash Tabasco sauce
  Celery salt and freshly ground black pepper to taste

Mix together all ingredients. Pour over ice in a 12-ounce brandy snifter. Garnish with a combination of the following: celery stick, scallion, pickled okra, banana pepper, cherry pepper, jalapeño pepper, and lime.

Dragon's Eye

YIELD: 1 SERVING

- 1 ounce vodka
- ½ ounce cranberry schnapps or cranberry liqueur
- 3 ounces cranberry juice
- 1 handful (approximately 4 ounces) ice
- 2 frozen grapes

Blend vodka, cranberry schnapps or liqueur, cranberry juice, and ice until thick. Pour into a 4-ounce martini glass and plop grapes on top for dragon's eyes. Stick in two straws on opposite side of grapes to resemble snout (it works!).

Lemon Drop

YIELD: 1 SERVING

1½ ounces vodka
½ ounce Triple Sec
Juice of ½ lemon
Ice
Lemon twist

Shake together all ingredients except lemon twist. Let stand to chill. Strain into 4-ounce martini glass, add lemon twist, and serve.

Pink Adobe Margarita

YIELD: 1 SERVING

Forty years ago, before the margarita became civilized and was served in a glass, we drank tequila using the technique attributed to Ernest Hemingway: a shot glass of tequila, some salt on your hand between your forefinger and thumb, and a wedge of lime. The technique was to lick the salt, take a bite of lime, and down the tequila in one swallow. Then someone in Tijuana, Mexico, invented a drink, called it *margarita* after a Hollywood starlet, and its fame became widespread. Today, every bar and almost every margarita aficionado has a margarita recipe. Here is the Pink Adobe's version.

1 ounce gold tequila (preferably Herradura)
¾ ounce Triple Sec or Grand Marnier
1½ ounces sweet and sour mix
½ ounce fresh lime juice
Ice
Salt
1 lime, cut into wedges

Combine tequila, Triple Sec, sweet and sour mix, and lime juice.

Shake with ice. Rub rim of large-bowled stemmed glass (12-ounce snifter) with cut lime. Dip glass in bowl of salt so that salt adheres to rim. Pour contents of shaker into glass. Garnish with lime wedge. For frozen margaritas, mix ingredients in blender with ice.

Pink Dream

YIELD: 1 SERVING

This and many other delectable Pink Adobe drinks were concocted—and meticulously tested—by longtime Pink bartender, Rob Higgins.

- ¾ ounce white crème de cacao
- ¾ ounce vodka
- 3 ounces (1 small scoop) raspberry sherbet
- 3 ounces (1 small scoop) vanilla ice cream
- 3 ounces ice

Blend all ingredients until thick and serve in a 7-ounce stemmed wineglass.

Mexican Chocolate

YIELD: 4 CUPS

3 ounces semisweet chocolate, shaved
3 tablespoons sugar
¼ teaspoon ground cinnamon
¼ teaspoon vanilla extract
3 cups milk

In a 2-quart saucepan, mix together all ingredients. Bring to a boil. When chocolate melts and mixture is boiling, beat with a rotary beater until boiling stops. Allow mixture to boil again, then beat again. Repeat this process one more time. The chocolate should be very frothy.

Rosalita

YIELD: 1 SERVING

1 ounce gold tequila
¾ ounce Triple Sec
1½ ounces cranberry juice
½ ounce fresh lime juice
Ice
¼ ounce Grand Marnier
1 slice lime

Shake together all ingredients except Grand Marnier and lime slice. Splash Grand Marnier on top and serve in a 7-ounce stemmed wineglass. Squeeze lime slice on top.

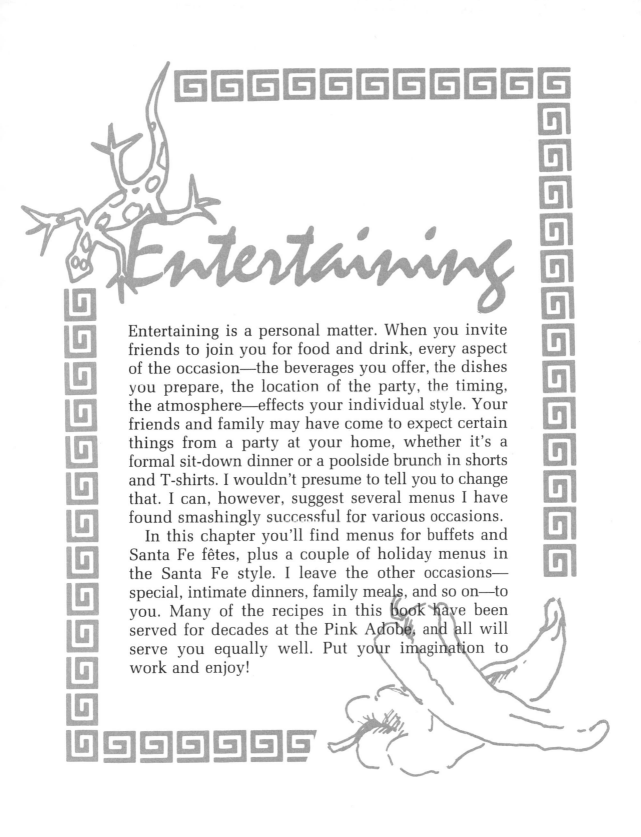

Entertaining

Entertaining is a personal matter. When you invite friends to join you for food and drink, every aspect of the occasion—the beverages you offer, the dishes you prepare, the location of the party, the timing, the atmosphere—effects your individual style. Your friends and family may have come to expect certain things from a party at your home, whether it's a formal sit-down dinner or a poolside brunch in shorts and T-shirts. I wouldn't presume to tell you to change that. I can, however, suggest several menus I have found smashingly successful for various occasions.

In this chapter you'll find menus for buffets and Santa Fe fêtes, plus a couple of holiday menus in the Santa Fe style. I leave the other occasions—special, intimate dinners, family meals, and so on—to you. Many of the recipes in this book have been served for decades at the Pink Adobe, and all will serve you equally well. Put your imagination to work and enjoy!

New Mexican-Style Intimate Buffet (For 10–12)

This menu is a distinct combination of meats and flavors—chicken, pork, and cheese—along with the intensity of the red and green chile.

Drinks
Sangritas (page 172)
Rosalitas (page 176)

Appetizers
Salsa Diabolique (page 22) with Chips
Nachos (page 4)

Buffet
Chicken Enchiladas with Sour Cream (page 82)
Red Chile with Pork (page 110)
Zucchini with Corn and Green Chiles (page 134)
Priscilla's Perfect Tamales (page 149)
Pink Adobe Guacamole (page 6) on Tomato Slices
Flour Tortillas (page 140)

Desserts
Margarita Pie (page 164)
Biscochitos (page 158)
Mexican Chocolate (page 176)

Place the salsa with chips and the nachos on a coffee table for the guests to serve themselves.

Arrange the hot food on a buffet table that has been decorated with fresh fruits and flowers. Serve the guacamole on tomato slices on a large platter that is garnished with watercress and cilantro. Make and serve the enchiladas in a bake and serve 9-by-12-inch pan. Serve the zucchini in a pretty 2-quart casserole dish. Serve the red chile and tamales in separate chafing dishes.

Place the Margarita Pie, Biscochitos, and Mexican Chocolate along with plates, forks, and mugs on a separate table.

Celebration Dinner (For 6)

For an anniversary, birthday, or getting a raise, this is a wonderful way to celebrate.

Drinks
Open Bar

Appetizers
Rosemary Walnuts (page 11)
Fiesta Caviar Pie (page 5)

Soup
Brie with Green Chile (page 26)

Main Course
Fabulous Braised Leg of Lamb (page 114)
Caramelized New Potatoes (page 126)
Buttered Parsley Asparagus (page 120)

Salad
Bibb Lettuce with Grilled Brie Toast (page 41)
(See note)

Dessert
Strawberries with Champagne (page 167)

NOTE: *Follow instructions for salad, but divide and serve on six individual plates.*

Fiesta Brunch
(For 6)

Drinks
Margaritas (page 174)
Lemon Drops (page 174)

Appetizers
Smoked Salmon Ball (page 8) with Crackers

Buffet
Turkey Mole Poblano (page 96)
Sopapillas (page 142) and/or
Green Chile Risotto (page 153)
Flour Tortillas (page 140)

Dessert
Lemon Meringue Pie (page 162)
Coffee

The salmon ball may be prepared the day before and refrigerated. Remove from refrigerator about an hour before serving to soften it for easy spreading. Place on coffee table or some other convenient place for guests to serve themselves while having cocktails.

Sopapilla is a fried bread very similar to the beignets of New Orleans. The dough for the sopapillas may be made ahead, but should be fried only when ready to serve, hot and fresh! The same is true for the risotto. Time it so that it does not have to wait for your guests—debut it at its prime.

Viva la fiesta!

Patio or Poolside Seafood Chalupa Party (For 8–10)

Drinks

Creole Marys (page 173)
Margaritas (page 174)

Buffet

3 dozen fresh corn tortillas (page 137)
Poached Salmon (page 74)
1 pound crabmeat, flaked and picked over carefully to remove shell and cartilage
½ pound lobster meat, cooked and flaked
3 cups black beans, cooked, seasoned, and mashed
1 cup goat cheese, crumbled
1 cup Green Chile Relish (page 19)
1 cup Mayonnaise (page 54), mixed with 1 teaspoon chopped pickled jalapeño pepper
2 cups peeled and chopped fresh tomatoes (page xiv)
2 avocados, peeled, pitted, and cut into ½-inch cubes
2 cups shredded lettuce

Deep-fry tortillas, one at a time, until crisp.

Place the poached salmon on a large platter. Garnish with cilantro leaves and lime slices.

Place all other ingredients in separate bowls—bright-colored stoneware pottery preferred.

Carefully place fried tortillas in a large, napkin-lined basket. Place in the center of table. Surround basket in a pleasing composition with the bowls of food and platter of salmon.

The guests make their own chalupas by taking a tortilla from the basket and topping it with any or all of the many choices.

Polo Picnic
(For 6)

Summertime brings polo to Santa Fe. This exciting game is eagerly awaited and well attended every Sunday afternoon. Many high goal players from all over the world have played in Santa Fe. The Pink Adobe sponsors a team that is very proudly called "the Pink Adobe Dragons." We like to watch and celebrate their victories while enjoying an elegant little picnic.

Basket of fruit - strawberries, peaches, and grapes
Turkey and Kidney Bean Salad (see page 51) in Pita bread
White Wine
Coffee

Slice off the tops of six pieces of Pita pocket bread and spread soft butter inside each with a rubber spatula. Instead of individual servings as done in the recipe for Turkey and Kidney Bean Salad, make it in one large bowl. Eliminate the two heads of lettuce that are called for and instead chop 2 or 3 leaves of romaine with ½ head leaf lettuce. Divide lettuce into each Pita bread and fill each with the Turkey and Kidney Bean Salad. Wrap each individually with plastic wrap and place in a picnic basket.

Mash the avocado and jalapeño together. Cover with plastic wrap. Put sour cream in one covered container and cheese in a plastic bag.

When ready to serve, top Pita sandwiches with avocado mixture, a dollop of sour cream, and a sprinkling of cheese. The fruit serves both as an appetizer and dessert. Take along a bottle or two of chilled white wine and a thermos of coffee.

Santa Fe Cocktail Buffet (For 15–20)

This informal menu has always proven to be successful for me. It is especially appropriate for early in the fall after viewing the autumn-colored aspens in the Sangre de Cristo mountains or for an après ski party.

Drinks
Open Bar

Cocktail Food
Peanut Chicken Wings (page 4)
Gingered Pork Cubes (page 10)
Salsa Diabôlique (page 22)
Priscilla's Perfect Tamales (page 149)
Shrimp Rémoulade (page 9, triple the recipe)
Muchos Frijoles Soup (page 30, triple the recipe)
Jalapeño Corn Bread (page 142, double the recipe)

Desserts
Fresh Fruit
Biscochitos (page 158)

Arrange the cocktail food on a buffet table well away from the bar where guests may serve themselves without engaging in a traffic jam. Serve the Shrimp Rémoulade in one large bowl with picks next to it for spearing the shrimp.

About halfway through the party, bring the soup to the table in a large chafing dish or tureen, along with the corn bread, bowls, and spoons.

Choose the fruit you prefer—a quart of strawberries with powdered sugar for dipping is loved by all.

Santa Fe Opera Tailgate Party (For 4-6)

Opera time in Santa Fe is eagerly anticipated all over the country by thousands of opera buffs. Opening night is always a gala affair, with dinner parties citywide. Among many Santa Feans it has become an almost ritualistic custom to plan a very elegant tailgate party, complete with china, crystal, silver, and linen. In their finest opera gowns, tails, and capes, they will bring folding chairs and enjoy a gourmet evening under the New Mexico skies while waiting for the performance to begin. This is a very familiar sight in the parking lot of the beautiful Santa Fe Opera.

Drinks
Champagne
Fiesta Caviar Pie (page 5)
Rocky Mountain Trout with Crabmeat Mayonnaise (page 74)
Sliced cucumbers with Dijon Dressing (page 53)

Desserts
Pralines (page 166)

NOTE: *Trout is served at room temperature. This can be prepared earlier in the day. Place on tray and cover with plastic wrap. Put Crabmeat Mayonnaise in container with lid. Place salad greens in bowl, cover with plastic wrap. Bring salad dressing along in a screwtop jar.*

A New Mexico Thanksgiving Dinner

YIELD: 6 TO 10 SERVINGS

One does not have to live in New Mexico to celebrate a New Mexican Thanksgiving. Break with tradition. Your family and friends will love it. Set the table with a gaily colored Mexican or Indian cloth. Fill a basket with fresh vegetables for a centerpiece. Try to find some piñon incense so that you may capture the "smell" of New Mexico.

Drinks
Pink Adobe Margaritas (page 174)

Appetizers
Chili Peanuts (page 8)
Santa Fe Layered Bean Dip (page 2)

Main Course
Turkey Mole Poblano (page 96)
Zucchini with Corn and Green Chiles (page 134)
Flour Tortillas (page 140)
Cranberry Relish (page 16)

Dessert
Southwestern Bread Pudding (page 159)
Mexican Chocolate (page 176)

Beverage suggestion: Cabernet Sauvignon or Dos Equis beer.

New Year's Eve Party

At the Pink Adobe our New Year's Eve party has become a tradition. After the clock has struck twelve, the whistles have been blown, the balloons released, and everyone has been kissed, we serve a bountiful buffet. Every year the menu is different, except for the black-eyed peas, which are always served to assure, as some believe, a following year of health, prosperity, and happiness.

Drinks
Champagne to toast the New Year
Open Bar

Buffet Table
Priscilla's Perfect Tamales (page 149)
Ham Glazed with Apricot (page 108)
Green Chili Relish (page 19)
Black-eyed Peas (page 128)

Dessert
Pralines (page 166)

NOTE: *Please take into account that most of the recipes are for 6 servings, so double or triple accordingly, with the exception of the ham. A 16-pound ham, sliced thin, will serve 20 to 25 persons when used as a filling for the biscuits.*

Index